THE NEW
CANADIAN
GARDEN

THE NEW CANADIAN GARDEN

MARK CULLEN

WITH MARETTE SHARP

DUNDURN
TORONTO

Editor: Allison Hirst
Design: Courtney Horner
Cover Design: Sarah Beaudin
Printer: Friesens

Library and Archives Canada Cataloguing in Publication

Cullen, Mark, 1956-, author
The new Canadian garden / Mark Cullen ; with Marette Sharp.

Includes index.
Issued in print and electronic formats.
ISBN 978-1-4597-3224-7 (paperback).--ISBN 978-1-4597-3225-4 (pdf).--
ISBN 978-1-4597-3226-1 (epub)

1. Gardening--Canada. I. Sharp, Marette, author II. Title.

SB453.3.C2C843 2016   635.0971   C2015-907327-8
                                               C2015-907328-6

1   2   3   4   5   20   19   18   17   16

We acknowledge the support of the **Canada Council for the Arts** and the **Ontario Arts Council** for our publishing program. We also acknowledge the financial support of the **Government of Canada** through the **Canada Book Fund** and **Livres Canada Books**, and the **Government of Ontario** through the **Ontario Book Publishing Tax Credit** and the **Ontario Media Development Corporation**.

Printed and bound in Canada.

VISIT US AT
Dundurn.com | @dundurnpress | Facebook.com/dundurnpress | Pinterest.com/dundurnpress

Dundurn
3 Church Street, Suite 500
Toronto, Ontario, Canada
M5E 1M2

IN MEMORY OF CANADA'S
FALLEN HEROES

As the volunteer chair of the Highway of Heroes Living Tribute Campaign it is a privilege to donate all of the author royalties from the sale of this book to the planting of 117,000 trees along Canada's Highway of Heroes (Trenton to Keele Street on Highway 401 in Ontario), one tree for each of Canada's war dead.

A living tribute to the greatest sacrifice and the greatest country in the world.

To learn more, please visit www.hohtribute.ca

— Mark Cullen

CONTENTS

INTRODUCTION

It is a bright morning in early summer and the tree swallows that have been nesting in my birdhouses have pushed their young out of their nests. Two of the youngsters, within earshot of my work desk, sit up on the eaves of our front porch. I can hear them complaining about how bossy their mother is. One looks at the other with indignation and chatters away. Then it's his sister's turn.

It seems like yesterday that the swallows arrived in my 10-acre garden to choose their abodes from the 27 nesting boxes that I had placed around the meadow. Like kids arriving for camp, they raced to their cabins to select their bunks. It was the third week of April: they arrive at precisely the same time each year, like clockwork. Birds of habit. And I am thankful for them. I love to watch their missile-shaped bodies dip and dive as they gather mosquitoes and other flying insects under their wings. Tree swallows have a wonderful iridescent blue/black coat with a white tummy: tiny tuxedoes worn to celebrate the gift of each day.

Ten weeks later, the adults have hatched their eggs, raised their young, and are now teaching them how to feed and fend for themselves.

Imagine if our lives were truncated down to a mere few weeks, from birth to being "pushed out of the nest." I understand that the average life expectancy for a Canadian songbird is two to three years, but they cram a lot of living into that short period of time.

Gardeners are fortunate: we tend to live a little longer. Anecdotally, I believe that we generally live longer than non-gardeners. It must be all of the exercise, fresh air, and closeness to nature that does it. Or maybe that's just wishful thinking on my part.

About 25 years ago I wrote the bestselling book *The Greener Thumb*, for Canadians who wanted a "complete guide to gardening in Canada," (as the subtitle announced). I won't be writing another *Greener Thumb*, I can tell you. As I browse through it now, I am reminded of just how much we have changed in a generation.

The New Canadian Garden takes a fresh approach to an old topic. As I reflect on the gardener's priorities in the 90s, I am reminded that gardening will never be that way again.

First, because newer homes are being built on much smaller lots than they were 25 years ago; in fact, many "homes" are not even houses at all, but condos, with intensely planned and planted balconies that present new opportunities and challenges.

Second (and more importantly), the incoming generation of gardeners has challenged all of us to look at gardening from a different point of view, with less concern for aesthetics and a greater focus

← Sempervivum growing on my green roof.

on food gardening and environmentally responsible planting and care.

Gone are the days of the rose gardens and peony collections (or lily, dahlia, or daylily collections). This is not to say that they do not exist, but it is highly unlikely that a new gardener will aim to collect plants as one collects stamps or coins. The 20-, 30-, and 40-somethings are much more likely to grow vegetables, herbs, and fruits in the yard and garden, the goal being to provide healthy foods for their table.

The incoming generation of gardeners are turning up the heat on environmental issues. They garden with an eye on biodiversity, attracting pollinators to their garden and balcony, and are demanding that more attention be paid to rebuilding our urban tree canopy.

Today's new gardeners are vocal and social. You may not find a busload of them at your local horticultural society meetings, but you will find them on Facebook and Pinterest and other social media outlets sharing pictures and experiences from their gardens. You will also find them in line-ups for allotment gardens or to participate in a local community garden each season.

The new Canadian gardener believes in sharing the green, growing world with their children and grandchildren (not all new Canadian gardeners are young adults), which is a great relief to those of us who worry about "nature deficit disorder" in kids (see page 157).

The new Canadian gardener often is a new Canadian — someone who brings the benefits of their gardening and farming experience from other parts of the world to their own yard and to community gardens here in Canada.

The Canadian garden has vastly changed over the years, and it is a very exciting place to be. I am delighted that you have picked up this book and I hope that you will benefit from every page as we journey together into the present, and the future, of gardening in Canada. As you read, you will discover that gardeners are birders, conservationists, environmentalists, parents, grandparents, family people, social people, and individuals who strive to make the world a better place, one plant at a time.

This is *The New Canadian Garden*. It is the most exciting time in the history of our country to be a gardener. I am grateful that the swallows have come back to remind me of that.

One of my tree swallows. →

FROM SEED
TO TABLE

CHAPTER ONE

It was buried treasure. With each turn of the garden fork, more of them were revealed. Emma shrieked with the appearance of every potato as I turned over the sandy loam. She grabbed each tuber with her chubby four-year-old hands and looked at every specimen with wonder: *Where did THIS come from? And why is it here?*

The experience confirmed all of the good things that I looked forward to when first faced with the prospect of parenthood. There are not enough precious moments like this in life and the memory lives in my mind like it happened yesterday, even though it was close to 24 years ago.

To fully experience the joy and mystery of life, we sometimes need to see it through the eyes of someone younger and less experienced. Kids are the best facilitators of this. Our preconceptions about how the world turns are set on their ear when we view them through the kaleidoscope of a child's mind.

And there is nothing that brings the generations together like food does.

I don't need to reflect on the many times that friends and family come together around the table to enjoy a good meal: there are countless recipe books out there to help you do that. My focus here is on growing food. Although there are not enough pages in this chapter to cover everything about this subject, I can give you an overview of the process, which will help get you started and keep you going for a while.

The goal here is to help you achieve the vision that you have for a productive and successful food garden or the integration of food crops into your ornamental garden, which is a growing trend among Canadian gardeners.

Thirty-five percent of Canadians currently grow some food in their gardens or on their balconies. While the sales of fruit trees and berry bushes are catapulting to new heights, tomatoes are, and I believe always will be, the most popular home-grown vegetable in Canadian gardens. But let's not forget the market-loving society we live in: Gardeners and non-gardeners alike have never been as keen on spending their Saturday morning at the farmers' market as they are today.

Why is this? I believe it all boils down to one simple thing: today's folks are interested in eating healthy food. Taking control of the growing process is the best way to ensure that the food we consume is of the best possible quality and contains as few chemicals as possible. Growing our own veggies, herbs, and fruit is the perfect excuse to get out of doors to enjoy some fresh air and engage in an experience that brings us one step closer to nature. Put another way, it is not computerized and it does not require the power provided by electrical outlets. Natural sunshine provides all of the energy that is needed to get the job done.

Food-growing is also liberating in a way that no other experience can be. Out there in my vegetable garden, I am not tethered to my cellphone if I don't want to be, and I am engaged in a process that produces something that is not only tasty, but good for me at the same time. I get a great deal of satisfaction from that.

My daughter Emma lives in London, England, now. She has a container of herbs on the front step of her rented flat, and she enjoys snipping fresh morsels off it for her table as she prepares a meal. Much more than that, she is a "foodie." At least every second day, she sends us pictures of meals she is preparing or has ordered at a restaurant. She loves food: shopping for it on weekends at her local farmers' market, preparing it for the table, and experimenting with it to create dishes that are uniquely hers. I do not believe that her experience in the potato garden as a youngster was life transforming. But I like to think of it as one guidepost in her life's journey that helped to shape her into the food-loving person that she is today.

Our experience in the vegetable garden almost a generation ago reminds me that this new phenomenon, and the sharp focus this generation has on food gardening, is as old as the ages. It is just more intense than before, and it is framed by both the limitations of space that new homeowners face today and the opportunities created by new gardening methods, technologies, and our interest in growing food in the absence of synthetic chemicals.

We still have to work hard at it to be successful, but then, as Jim Nollman says in his book *Why We Garden*, "Gardening is hard work; it doesn't make life easier, although it often makes it more fulfilling."

In Canada, growing food on a small scale can be traced back to the two tribes of the Iroquois, the Huron-Wendat and the Mohawk, who took part in a more sedentary farming lifestyle than the nomadic one of the Algonquin. Rather than following their food, the Iroquois grew their own. This allowed them to build more permanent structures and develop a deeper understanding of agriculture. These tribes continued the hunting and gathering lifestyle while practising an early form of agriculture, mainly employing the use of the "Three Sisters": maize, beans, and squash. We can thank the First Nations for introducing Europe to these food plants about 500 years ago.

The vegetables that make up the "Three Sisters" all have something to contribute: Maize is the tallest and provides shade for the squash and a vertical pole for the beans to climb up. Beans, being legumes, replenish the soil's nitrogen reserves. Squash covers the soil, preventing the growth of weeds that would otherwise compete for space, water, and nutrients. Today we call this "companion planting," and the Three Sisters method is still in use.

← Corn, beans, and squash work together when planted closely. This "Three Sisters" method of planting was employed by Native North Americans years ago and is still practised today.

WHY DO WE GROW FOOD?

It seems like an easy question with a simple answer: we grow food to survive. After all, we need food to fuel our bodies, to supply our tissues with moisture, nutrients, and vitamins to move, grow, repair, and think. Beyond that, though, beyond the necessity that engulfs the process, why do a third of Canadians engage in food gardening when the majority of us generally have easy access to a wide variety?

Gardening for food is more than a means to an end. It is a time to *play in the dirt*, to let the soil run through your hands, to not feel guilty when you get dirty; it is the thrill of watching those seeds, tiny and seemingly insignificant, emerge from the ground and grow a little every day; it is knowing where your food comes from, where it's been, and appreciating the effort it took to get it here. Above all else, it helps us to understand how connected we are with Mother Nature and how dependent on her we are for survival — not the other way around.

I get a thrill out of growing food in my garden each spring and summer. I guess that's why I carved an acre out of our property for this purpose!

According to a National Gardening Association Special Report, the number one reason that we grow our own food, though, is to produce something that *tastes better* than what we can buy. This does not surprise me, as I have purchased some pretty tasteless tomatoes from the grocery store.

Also on the list: financial savings, increased food quality and safety, being able to eat more locally, and getting more exercise and time outdoors. But are these all good reasons to "grow your own"?

Financially speaking, I'm inclined to say yes. Not only do you save money at the grocery store, you will likely avoid excessive car trips in search of fresh produce, money on plastic bags when you forget your reusables, and I personally find that less goes to waste when I'm growing my own: I just can't throw away something I worked so hard to produce.

↑ My harvest of heritage veggies — a moment of pride.

My hand: my dirt (teeming with life!). →

Not convinced? Here are some numbers. If you grow one tomato plant, and one pepper plant, and you do a good job of it, you will spend just over $3.50 for the seeds. In return, you will yield about $45 in produce. Not a bad investment opportunity, if you ask me!

Many of the supplies you need are one-time purchases that last quite a long time: pots, tools, fertilizer (and if you compost, the fertilizer is free). Note that your soil will need to be amended each season and it is impossible to put a value on that. Seed packets come with an average of 10 seeds and, assuming you keep them in a cool, dry place, they can last several years.

The quality and safety of our food has become increasingly important to us. Food quality includes, of course, what you expect to see on food store shelves, how the food smells and feels in your hand. When you're eating it, how does it taste? What are its nutritional qualities? How was it produced?

Today's consumers seem to be shifting gears: to a greater degree than ever we don't want to give up valuable nutrition and taste for something that looks perfect. Some Canadian consumers are quite willing to grab the tomato that looks a little beat-up if she knows it was grown in a sustainable manner. With the widespread use of chemicals to ward off insect pests and disease, we have sacrificed food safety for aesthetics. Growing your own food puts you in control of your food's safety and quality.

🍁 EAT LOCALLY

Canadians love their locally produced food. Look at the number of farmers' markets that have sprung up across the country for evidence of this. Today, even in the city, we only need to go as far as our backyard, patio, balcony, or local community or allotment garden for fresh, safe, and tasty vegetables and fruit.

With the right tools and know-how, you can easily grow great food in your own yard, or on your balcony or patio. Of course, exercise and time outdoors go hand-in-hand. Sure, the hammock is inviting on those sweltering mid-August days, but relaxation for me is also getting out into my garden, weeding, hoeing, picking, and, sometimes, eating right on the spot. To pull a carrot and wipe it on my pant leg only to munch down

on it right there — now, that is paradise! I can enjoy a walk through the urban allotment garden (when someone leaves the gate open) for inspiration and energy.

Thirty-five percent of Canadians grow their own food. That statistic tells us a lot about us. While the reasons will vary as to why they choose to do so, there are millions of people benefiting from the many positive qualities the simple act of growing our own food carries with it. For the 65 percent of Canadians who have not started growing their own food, there is no time like the present to get growing!

It is true that gardening is not without its physical challenges; my experience tells me that we can condition ourselves to them over time. I'll quote Jim Nollman again: "Gardening is hard work; it doesn't make life easier, although it often makes it more fulfilling."

↑ Weeding: the second most important job after planting.

❧ UNDERSTANDING AND MAXIMIZING YOUR SPACE

I'm rather fond of referring to the potential gardening areas of your home as "your space." My space is different from yours and yours is different from that of your neighbour. You may choose to garden solely on your patio, while your mother chooses to rip out her lawn and replace it with edible plants. We are all different in our gardening preferences, and so in this section I will show you several different potential uses for your outdoor spaces.

Every yard (and patio or deck) comes with its benefits and challenges. Understanding what those are right from the get-go will speed things up down the road and minimize potential problems. For simplicity's sake, I lay out the pros and cons for each as well as offer a few suggestions for overcoming obstacles to your success. As you read through the following chart, consider your space and make a list of your own pros and cons. What does your space offer in terms of light, moisture, and soil quality? How will you overcome any challenges posed by your particular space?

↑ A not-so-random act of colour.

In fall, rake fallen leaves off lawns and into your garden beds. →

SPACE CONSIDERATIONS

Type of Space	Pros	Cons	Solutions/Options
YARD	1. Soil is already available. 2. Permanent watering systems are easy to install. 3. Soil stays moist for longer than in pots. 4. Can use raised beds to improve soil quality, ease of access, and reduce the amount of site preparation. 5. If yard is large enough, you can plant fruit trees; if another fruit tree of the same species is located within sixty metres, you will only need to plant one; choose dwarf rootstocks.	1. Site preparation can be laborious (removing grass, weeds, stumps). 2. Using the same soil every year increases the potential for pests and diseases (you will need to amend it with generous quantities of compost or composted manure). 3. Yard trees may provide too much shade. 4. Soil may be contaminated (which will require that you remove it and replace it with quality triple mix).	1. Consider installing a raised bed; smother the future garden area with plywood, several layers of newspaper, or thick (six millimetre) black plastic to kill off anything growing beneath (this will take up to six weeks); lightly till the area and keep on top of weeding once plants have been transplanted; consider using greenhouse-grown transplants the first year to give them a quick, sure start; use a sharp hoe to cut down weeds easily. 2. Crop rotation can play a huge role in combating these problems. See the section on crop rotation for some simple ideas; encourage healthy soil by removing infected plants and throwing them away (not in the composter). 3. If yard trees are completely shading your property, try growing plants that do not require as much sun. See page 32 for shade-tolerant crops. 4. There's always potential for contaminated soil, so it's a good idea to get it tested.
PATIO	1. Can be completely exposed to the sun, causing quick drying (but ideal conditions for "sun-seeking" plants!). 2. Can use a mix of pots and planters placed for different effects. 3. Can make use of railings and unused vertical space like fences and walls. 4. Close to house and perhaps the kitchen — more likely that the veggies and herbs will be used if they are closer to the kitchen.	1. A covered patio or one located on the north side of a house can provide too much shade. 2. Pots and planters dry out faster than ground soil.	1. Choose to plant vegetables and herbs that don't require very much sun. See page 32 for shade-tolerant crops. 2. Use self-watering pots and check moisture levels daily. Be sure to allow soil to dry about three centimetres deep between watering.

SPACE CONSIDERATIONS			
Type of Space	**Pros**	**Cons**	**Solutions/Options**
BALCONY	1. Railings provide added space to hang planters and small pots — great for herbs and veggies that don't need deep soil. 2. Plants will be able to take advantage of heat radiating from walls — allows you to start plants earlier. 3. Close to house and perhaps the kitchen — more likely that the veggies and herbs will be used if they are closer to the kitchen.	1. Weight restrictions. 2. Light: an issue depending on which direction balcony faces and buildings next to yours that may block sunlight. 3. Wind and temperature fluctuations increase as you move higher. Any storey above the third floor will likely be exposed to higher than average wind on a regular basis. 4. Balcony railings and walls may provide too much shade, especially when facing north or northeast.	1. Know and understand the weight restrictions of the building; always leave a little wiggle room and account for weight of wet soil which weighs considerably more than dry soil. 2. Observe the light your balcony receives and take note; if your balcony receives very little sun, choose to plant veggies and herbs that don't require a lot of light. See page 32 for shade-tolerant crops. 3. Wind dries out plants faster. Choose deep, self-watering containers and mulch your containers with weed-free, finely ground up cedar bark mulch. 4. If your balcony railings are shading the balcony floor where pots and planters are located, raise the pots up so they receive the maximum amount of sun and air circulation under the pot at the root zone.
ROOF	1. Plenty of sun. 2. A good use of space that may otherwise go unused. 3. Soil catches rainwater rather than allowing it to flow off the roof.	1. Weight restrictions. 2. Can be expensive if you are installing a larger unit. 3. Dry out quickly. 4. Some work may be involved in meeting safety standards according to municipality.	1. Know and understand the weight restrictions of the building; always leave a little wiggle room and account for weight of wet soil. 2. Rather than installing an entire green roof consider choosing containers. 3. The greater the soil mass in a pot or container the less frequently plants require water. Consider using the largest possible pots and containers for this reason (keeping in mind the weight factor!); monitor weather and soil moisture daily.

I garden in a yard. I actually have a 10-acre garden (when I include my three acres of meadows) of which one acre is vegetable garden and another half acre is fruit trees. I use the soil that is naturally located there and amend it each year with a fresh layer of compost mixed with 30 percent builder's or "sharp" sand. When planting certain heavy feeders like tomatoes, I add one part worm castings to five parts compost or triple mix. The worm castings add valuable microbes to the soil, charging it with a high rate of nutrition.

Note that I add compost to my planting beds every year. I also rake fallen leaves onto my flower and veggie beds each fall, but I rake them off my lawn where they can cause brown/dead patches. By the end of each growing season, existing plants have depleted the nutrients from the soil: I use the compost to replenish and feed the soil and the sharp sand to open up the soil to improve drainage. By the way, I have a naturally alkaline, clay-based soil on my property, as most Southern Ontarians do.

Crop Rotation

Listening and watching good farmers can be quite informative! A good farmer practises crop rotation to keep soil nutrient levels balanced and pesky bugs confused. The basic idea is that from year to year you are moving the crops to a different spot in the garden. Each crop uses different quantities of the available nutrients, so crop rotation helps to maximize the performance of each crop that you plant. Certain crops *return* nutrients to the soil just by living (legumes, for example, are able to convert nitrogen from an unusable form to a useable one).

← Peas are members of the legume family. They increase usable nitrogen in the soil.

Year 1	**Year 2**	**Year 3**	**Year 4**

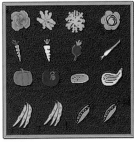 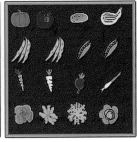 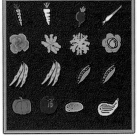 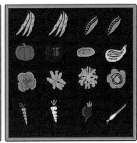

← This diagram shows the four-year rotation using the "leaves, fruits, roots, and legumes" method. You will not likely plant all of these vegetables I have outlined here, but it gives you a few examples of each type within the four categories. **Leaves:** lettuce, spinach, kale, chard, corn; **fruits:** tomato, pumpkin, potato, squash and cucurbits, sweet and hot pepper; **roots:** carrots, parsnips, radishes, onions, beets, garlic, ginger; **legumes:** beans, peas, peanuts, and lentils.

Even by moving the crops a few metres away from where they were the previous year, you are helping to create a positive living and growing environment. There are certain rotation combinations that work really well (see page 18 for details) and there are others that you should avoid, either because one crop cannot tolerate the residues left behind by another or the two crops require the same nutrients and will compete. These rotations that work are referred to as companion planting, a centuries-old technique that is well worth your consideration when planning a veggie garden each season.

For example, in my garden, I never plant the tomatoes in the same soil two years in a row. Even though I amend the soil each year, spores from powdery mildew and blight can reside in the soil. Sure, the spores can blow in from other gardens, but if they're harbouring in your own garden, your plants don't stand a chance.

To keep track of my garden's plan, I draw a very simple map. It doesn't matter how small your garden may be, the fact is that you won't likely remember where everything was come spring. I throw in some stable pieces (rocks, trees, buildings) so I can orientate my map, and then, over the winter, I use it to create a whole new plan.

As a "sustainable" gardener, it is important to understand that soil is a complex colony of interdependent living organisms that rely on raw, natural material to sustain it in good health. This is where the compost comes in.

TRIPLE MIX

What is "triple mix"? I often recommend triple mix as an all-purpose soil mixture for use when planting most anything in your garden (except in containers). It is generally accepted that it is made of equal portions top soil, peat (or peat moss), and compost (or composted cattle/steer manure). However, there are many variations of quality to triple mix. Some suppliers will skimp on the portion of compost and peat (the more expensive ingredients), use manure that is not properly composted, or top soil that is merely scraped from the surface of a farmer's field and is possibly laden with weed seeds and/or agricultural chemicals.

My advice is that you buy from a soil supplier that you know and trust to provide quality product. "Shake the hand of your soil supplier" is not a bad motto! Know him, or her, and don't be afraid to pay a premium price for the "good stuff."

The Basics

You can group all vegetables (or fruits) into four categories based on their growing habits.

Leaves and Stems: characterized by their leafy structure, we often do not eat the flowers and focus our attention on keeping these plants from flowering to avoid bolting; these include: broccoli, lettuce, cauliflower, kale, and spinach

Fruits and Seeds: these are the plants whose flowers turn into the parts of the plant we eat and require either self- or cross-pollination to produce a fruit: tomatoes, peppers, corn, and squash

Roots and Bulbs: the parts most often eaten grow underground; for example: onions, garlic, carrots, and beets

Legumes: a subsection of the fruits and seeds category, legumes produce a flower, which, when pollinated, grows into a fruit with seeds. The difference, though, is that legumes can return nitrogen to the soil and are separated into their own category so they can be rotated at the appropriate time; examples include: peas, green beans, peanuts, and lentils

It's best to have a little from each category to avoid the potential problems of monocropping. You can start each plot or row anywhere in the cycle. Just remember: leaves, fruits, roots, and legumes.

If you want to get into more detail, consider not just how the plant grows but the family to which it belongs. Tomatoes and potatoes, for example, are in the same family (Solanaceae) while beets and broccoli are in the same family (Brassicas). Despite the fact that tomatoes grow aboveground and potatoes grow underground, they use up the same nutrients in producing the edible part of the plant. See page 20-21 for plant families that can be planted together but not in the same soil two years in a row.

I recommend that you top up your garden soil every year with some finished compost or composted manure. When you amend the soil in this way you minimize the risk of spreading insects and disease through your garden. Combine soil amendment with crop rotation and you will experience optimum conditions for plant growth and productivity and minimize insect and disease problems.

HELPFUL CROP ROTATION TIPS

1. After legumes, plant a nitrogen-loving crop like those in the Brassicas family; avoid root vegetables as they will use the nitrogen to produce leaves rather than roots.

2. Plant root vegetables in soil that was previously used for heavy feeders, like the Solonaceae and Brassicas families.

3. Harvesting potatoes disturbs the soil structure, so consider planting root vegetables (Umbeliferae family) and onions (Allium family) after potatoes.

4. Perennial crops like strawberries, rhubarb, and asparagus should be given their own plot and should not be included in the rotation.

5. Salad greens can be grown anywhere there is room. Don't fuss too much about keeping them rotated.

6. Crop rotation is an effective prevention for club root, a disease that affects members of the Brassicas family. It is characterized by yellowing leaves, easy wilting, stunted growth, and poor plant formation, leading to death. Once the disease is present in the soil, it takes upwards of 20 years for it to die off. Best to just avoid this one.

FLOATING ROW COVERS

Interested in maximizing yield and minimizing insect damage? Try a "floating row cover" (pictured right) when you plant out your vegetables this spring. The white spun-polyester material allows the sun in and air and water to filter through to maximize growth. Best of all, due to the physical barrier, adult insects, like the cabbage moth, flea beetle, aphid, cutworm, and other caterpillars cannot access your valuable vegetables as they mature. It is a simple, inexpensive, and effective solution. A floating row cover minimizes the need for pesticides, too.

← These beans became overrun with earwigs due to the cool, wet spring. The earwigs damaged the cotyledon before the first true leaves could become established, causing the bean plant to wither and die.

THE VEGETABLE
FAMILIES

Fabaceae Family

peas
beans
lentils
peanuts

Allium Family

onion
garlic
shallot
chive
leek

Solanaceae Family

eggplant
potato
tomato
sweet pepper
hot pepper

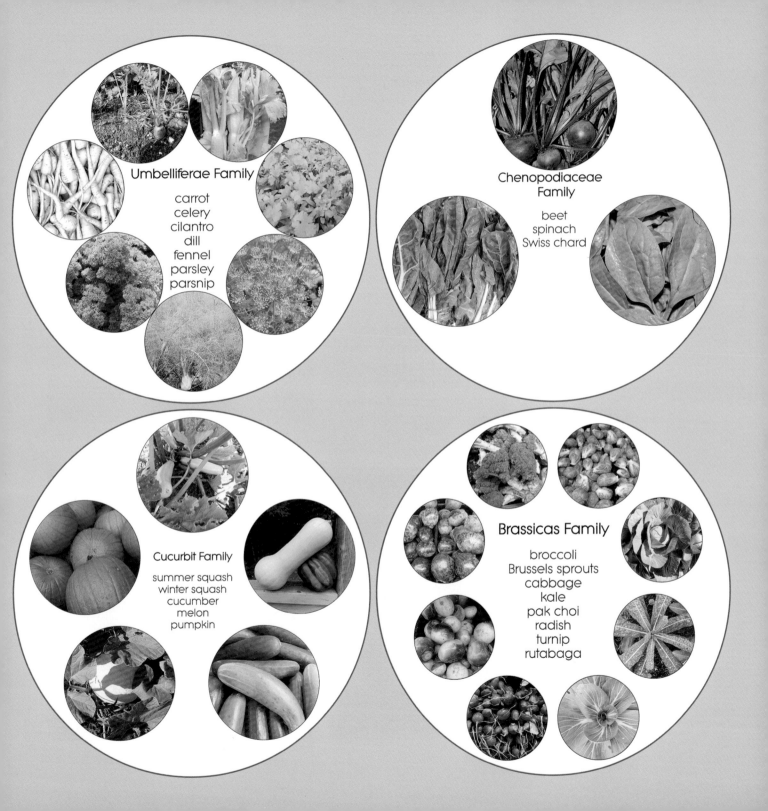

Umbelliferae Family

carrot
celery
cilantro
dill
fennel
parsley
parsnip

Chenopodiaceae Family

beet
spinach
Swiss chard

Cucurbit Family

summer squash
winter squash
cucumber
melon
pumpkin

Brassicas Family

broccoli
Brussels sprouts
cabbage
kale
pak choi
radish
turnip
rutabaga

Intercropping and Mixed Cropping

For very small gardens, using rows or plots and crop rotation may not be possible. If this is the case, intercropping or mixed cropping may be your best option. Choosing plants that are compact allows you to grow more. When I'm planning a small garden, I tend to think about two factors: how much room a plant will need and how long it will take to grow. Slow-growing and space-hogging plants are automatically out. The following plants fall into this category: asparagus, Brussels sprouts, celery, non-climbing squash varieties, main crop potatoes, parsnips, pumpkins, leeks, and corn.

On large-scale farms, intercropping is the practice of growing more than one crop in a field. Often done in an effort to increase yields, promote soil health, and encourage the "good" bugs, intercropping can be accomplished easily in the small home garden. Mixed cropping is similar,

Using the Three Sisters → (corn, bean, and squash), you can see how intercropping differs from mixed cropping. Either method promotes a healthy crop system, encouraging beneficial interaction between the species.

INTERCROPPING

Mixed Intercropping: When two or more crops are grown in a random arrangement. Generally there are no rows and crops are intermixed with one another.

Row Intercropping: When two or more crops are grown in rows with each row's direct neighbour being a different crop.

Strip Intercropping: When two or more crops are grown in rows but plants are spaced far enough apart to allow mechanical harvest, should it be desired, but close enough that they can interact with each other to improve yield of at least one of the crops.

Relay Intercropping: When two or more crops are grown together, but not started together. The second crop is planted into the first as it matures. This is particularly useful in the short Canadian growing season.

Intercropping

Mixed Cropping

except there are usually no rows of a single species; instead, they are mixed within the same row.

Intercropping is fairly simple, and with a small garden plot it can be done effectively since all crops can be reached without having to step over (or on) other plants. The traditional rows of a farmer's field, or your neighbour's large garden plot, leave empty spaces where weeds can grow and moisture goes unused. Planting these empty spaces with crops that do not take too much from the soil is a good way to intensify the yield and create less work for you (like weeding!). Plants that produce an edible product quickly, like radishes and leaf lettuce, shade the area, keeping the soil from drying out too quickly, and out-compete weeds without competing with the main crop.

Here are a few intercropping and mixed cropping tips. Please refer to the section on companion planting for ideas about what grows well together and what does not.

← Planting marigolds deters rodents and aphids.

1. Legumes can be planted beside plants that are heavy nitrogen feeders. Members of the Brassicas and Solonaceae families benefit from added nitrogen in the soil.

2. Plant marigolds and geraniums in or around your garden to deter rodents and aphids.

3. Do not plant so densely that air flow is reduced drastically. This can increase the spread of fungal diseases, many of which rely on lengthy periods of moisture to thrive.

4. Think about the root systems. Tomatoes and potatoes have deep root systems, whereas lettuce and spinach have shallow roots. They can occupy similar spaces without interfering with one another.

5. Focus on plant health before trying to force too many plants into a small space: do not compromise the health of a few plants by planting too many.

↑ Beans and tomatoes grow well together.

Square-Foot Gardening

Square-foot gardening is similar to intercropping, but with a little more structure. The basic idea is to use a raised bed (see page 26 to build your own) and divide it into equal square-foot portions. Within each of these squares, plant something different. The squares help to organize your garden bed and each plant is given enough space to grow without hindering itself or others.

Square-foot gardening is a great way to engage kids who can be given their own square to organize and manage. It's the perfect time to teach them, in an interactive way, about time management and planning ahead. Each crop has different needs depending on a few factors: its size at maturity, how

SPACING REQUIREMENTS FOR POPULAR GARDEN VEGGIES: SQUARE-FOOT GARDENING				
Crop	Spacing (inches)	# of Seeds/ Square Foot	Minimum Light Requirements (hours)	Notes
Carrot	2	36	4	Carrots grown in containers are limited in length by the height of the container, therefore container depth is more important than container width.
Bean (bush)	4	9	6	Think about how many beans you and your family can reasonably eat. Just because you can plant nine seeds, doesn't mean you have to. One bean plant will produce enough beans for two people if picked every few days.
Broccoli	3	16	4	Broccoli is a cool season crop, but you can still stagger the plantings so you don't have your entire broccoli crop ready at once.
Swiss chard	6	4	3	These are heavy producers in the right soil. Young leaves can grow well with three hours of sun. Give them more sunlight if you'd like more mature leaves.
Spinach	2	36	3	There are lots of varieties of spinach. Some have a spreading habit that fill out containers nicely.
Cucumber	12	1-2	6	Cucumber plants are a vine and can hang over the side of your raised bed.
Leaf lettuce	6	4	2	Depending on the type of leaf lettuce, you will be able to get more than four into a plot, especially if you will be picking it before maturity.
Head lettuce	12	1	3	Prone to earwig infestations, which is why they require more space than leaf lettuce. Sprinkle diatomaceous earth around the plant to keep earwigs away.
Onion	2	36	4	For large onions, space them farther apart. Remember, you're not spacing for the aboveground green matter but the belowground vegetable.
Peas	1	8	4	Technically, you can put 144 pea seeds in a square foot, but that doesn't mean you should. Eight is recommended as the maximum number and two to three plants will be plenty for a family of five.

it is pollinated, its root system, its need for nutrients, and its susceptibility to disease. To give you an idea of how they fit into a square-foot garden, the top homegrown crops are shown in the table below. Always read the seed package — most seed companies print spacing requirements, when to sow and plant out in the garden, and date to maturity (harvest). Take the days to maturity with a grain of salt, as they are very dependent on weather conditions. It gives you a good approximation, though.

Be reasonable with your planting. Think about how much you or your family will eat, and remember that just because a square can hold 36 radishes, doesn't mean you need to fill that entire square with radishes. Use a quarter of the space and plant nine radishes; use the remaining three-quarters for carrots or onions.

SPACING REQUIREMENTS FOR POPULAR GARDEN VEGGIES: SQUARE-FOOT GARDENING

Crop	Spacing (inches)	# of Seeds/ Square Foot	Minimum Light Requirements (hours)	Notes
Radish	2	36	4	Thin out radishes if they end up too close to one another or if you are planting larger radishes. Give them space to grow but remember that most are ready to pick within 45 days of germination.
Tomato	18	1	6	Provide ample room for tomatoes to improve airflow which will decrease chances of diseases.
Hot pepper	9		6	Hot peppers often produce more peppers per plant than sweet peppers.
Potato	12	1	4	Potatoes tend to trail off, plant them slightly closer to an edge to give them more room to send out new growth.
Sweet potato	12	1	6	Sweet potatoes like it hot. Plant near a building that will radiate heat back down to the plant.
Peanut	6	4	6	A great crop for returning nitrogen to the soil. Use after tomatoes, peppers, potatoes, or other heavy feeders. They need at least a foot of well-drained soil to perform well.
Sweet pepper	18	1	6	Sweet peppers do well with a little staking, especially when they have several peppers hanging from their stems.
Kale	8	1-2	4	Many kale varieties like to grow outwards and will take up the full eight inches you've allotted them; however, overlapping leaves isn't a problem.
Bean (pole)	4	9	6	Pole beans will need staking. Use a trellis attached directly to the raised bed or push poles into the soil.
Leek	4	9	4	Continue to push soil up around the leek stem to give it that sharp white/green contrast that leeks are known for.
Zucchini	24	1	6	Allow zucchini to travel over the side of the raised bed. Use a lattice to keep it from getting stepped on.

BUILDING YOUR OWN 4-FOOT X 4-FOOT RAISED BEDS

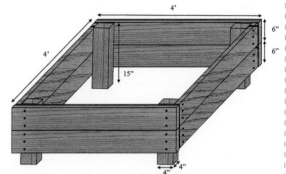

YOU WILL NEED:

- 8 X 2" x 6" x 4' boards (untreated)
- 4 X 4" x 4" x 15" posts
- 3.5" deck screws
- Saw
- Drill

1. Start by cutting your pieces to length.

2. Screw one 2"x 6" board onto one of the posts, keeping it flush with the top of the post. Attach another post to the opposite end of the board, again keeping it flush with the top.

3. Attach a second 2"x 6" board below the first, keeping the boards as close to one another as possible.

4. Do this a second time with the other two posts and four more boards.

5. Attach the two sides together using more boards on each end, closing off the square. You may find it easier to lay the entire thing upside down on a flat surface to keep it level.

6. Once complete, you should have a square with four posts that can be dug into the ground to keep the unit from moving.

7. Place your raised bed and fill it with really good soil. Plant away as soon as temperatures are above freezing!

The "ordered" → appearance of this allotment will soon collapse as plants and weeds begin to grow.

A proud moment in the autumn garden.. →

Companion Planting

Before doing any planting, draw up a plan. You might be thinking that this is just extra work and that you can plant anything anywhere you want. There is risk in this "fly by the seat of the pants" approach, however. For instance, when you plant garlic next to peas, your garlic will turn out to be all green and no bulb (i.e., no garlic). Companion planting is considered an art before a science. It is very important when planting in tight quarters, as each plant has a positive or negative effect on its neighbour. The **Companion Planting Chart** below will give you an idea of who gets along well with whom and who needs to be separated. As you plan your gardens, whether they are on balconies, in boxes, or right in the ground, check back with this reference to keep all your plants happy and healthy.

Companion Planting Chart

	Bean (bush)	Bean (pole)	Beets	Broccoli	Carrot	Cucumber	Dill	Head Lettuce	Hot Pepper	Kale	Leaf Lettuce	Leek	Onion	Peanut	Peas	Potato	Radish	Spinach	Sweet Pepper	Sweet Potato	Swiss Chard	Tomato	Zucchini
Bean (bush)			✓	✓	✓			✗	✗		✗	✗			✓	✓					✓		
Bean (pole)			✗	✓			✓	✗	✗	✓	✗	✗	✗							✗			
Beets	✓	✗		✓	✓		✓															✗	
Broccoli	✓	✓	✓			✓	✓	✗	✗	✓	✗								✗				
Carrot	✓					✓	✓	✓	✓		✓	✓	✓	✓	✓	✓	✓	✓	✓			✓	✓
Cucumber	✓			✓	✓		✓							✗	✓							✓	
Dill			✓	✓	✓																	✓	✓
Head Lettuce		✓	✓	✗	✓								✓										
Hot Pepper	✗	✗		✗																	✓	✓	
Kale	✗	✗	✓																✗			✗	
Leaf Lettuce		✓	✓	✗	✓																		
Leek	✗	✗												✗									
Onion	✗	✗	✓	✓	✓			✓			✓			✗	✗		✓			✓		✓	
Peanut		✗	✓		✓							✗											
Peas	✓				✓		✓				✓	✗	✗										
Potato	✓			✓	✓	✗							✓	✓								✗	✓
Radish					✓	✓		✓			✓		✓										
Spinach					✓								✓										
Sweet Pepper			✗	✓					✗				✓								✓	✓	
Sweet Potato							✓																
Swiss Chard	✓	✗											✓										
Tomato			✗	✓	✓	✓	✓	✓	✗				✓			✗							
Zucchini						✓									✓								

THE FIVE BENEFITS PROVIDED BY COMPANION PLANTING

1. *Distraction*: sometimes it's easier to plant an insect's favourite food away from their second-favourite food. The scent of this favoured treat will lure the insects away — just make sure you plant enough to keep them occupied. Nasturtiums are often planted around a veggie garden for this reason (to attract aphids away from other favourites).

2. *Harbouring an Army*: an army of the good bugs, that is. Certain plant species are real bug magnets, attracting aphid-munching syrphid flies (also called hover-flies or flower flies), ladybugs, and lacewings; parasitic wasps to control earwigs, slugs, and caterpillars; minute pirate bugs to devour mites; assassin bugs for just about every insect pest; and so many more. Or add flowering plants to attract pollinators, increasing the potential for the pollination of your edibles.

3. *Soil Amendments*: some plants make the soil better. Legumes convert atmospheric nitrogen and return it to the soil in a form that can be used by other plants; cover crops reduce erosion, prevent nutrient leaching, and add nutrients back into the soil when they are cut down and lightly tilled in. For non-farmers, cover crops are simply crops that are planted to keep the soil in place by keeping erosion from wind and water at bay. They do not remove a large amount of nutrients from the soil and will often replace lost nutrients. For more information about what crops will work best for your situation, see the Resource Guide for a great tool put out by Cornell University.

4. *Support*: like the Three Sisters (page 6), where corn and beans were planted together, one plant provides support and stability for another.

5. *Shelter*: just like it sounds — one larger plant providing shade and shelter from winds and heavy rains. Think again of the Three Sisters: squash was sheltered by the corn and climbing beans.

↑ Syrphid fly pollinating. We need more of them.

PATIO AND BALCONY GARDENS

The Patio Garden

A patio area is a great space to sit outside. Whether by yourself or with friends, the accessibility and relaxation provided by a patio is rarely matched. So why not start a little functional patio greening by adding some pots and planters filled with your favourite veggies? Makes sense to me!

They key to patio gardening is to understand the light your patio receives and to work with it rather than fight against it. There's no use planting peppers and tomatoes if your patio is shaded most of the day. Working with the natural elements will make your garden experience more enjoyable and your harvests more productive. Observe your patio space and make note of the sunniest areas: usually those that face south and west. If you notice plants starting to stretch for the sun, give them more by moving them. That's the beauty of patio gardening: nothing is static.

The Balcony Garden

Ah, the balcony garden. Whether you're at the top of a 70-storey high-rise or the second-storey of a cozy duplex, the balcony is your escape to the outside world. It may not get much use in the winter, but from spring to fall, refreshing mornings and warm evenings are spent on the balcony chatting with friends and family or just sitting with a good book.

Learning to use your balcony as a garden provides both challenges and opportunities. The space, plant weight, light, and (depending on how many stories up you are) wind are all factors that need to be considered. We have discussed the issue of space previously in the Patio Garden section and I will touch upon the most important factors again here.

Balcony Space

Like the small yard garden and patio, the balcony garden is all about space management. You want to be able to enjoy it, but also grow delicious vegetables and fruits in that space. Planning and organization are key, but also remember that, much like the patio garden, nothing is fixed, so pots and planters can be moved around if you find they're just not in quite the right place.

Balconies are often the smallest spaces to work with, which only means you have to be fastidious with your decisions. Choose one or two crops to grow (tomatoes and lettuce, for example). And be sure to choose something you eat plenty of. Browse the seed racks at your garden retailer and peruse the many online catalogues available. Do this early in the season for the widest possible selection.

Weight Restrictions

The balcony garden is limited not only by space but by weight restrictions set out for the specific balcony. This is ***extremely important*** to consider, as your safety overrides my desire to see you grow your own food. If you don't know how much weight your balcony can hold, contact your condominium or apartment management. Once you have a tangible number to work with, the rest is easy.

Always factor in the weight of wet soil: you will be watering your plants frequently. Consider the weight of the pots: plastic and Styrofoam are lightweight materials; clay and ceramic are heavy. If your container material absorbs water (wood, for example), be sure to account for that extra weight.

RECOGNIZING SIGNS OF SOIL DEFICIENCY

When the soil is deficient in one or more necessary elements for healthy plant growth, there are usually telltale signs. It might not be obvious at first, but over time you will begin to see your plants struggling. I would recommend some natural amendments (compost, for example) to ensure long-term success. Below is a comprehensive table of symptoms and the possible corresponding nutrient deficiencies.

Often the patio garden will do just fine without too much added fertilizer. I encourage you to use all new soil each spring when planting in containers. The soil from the previous year is good, just not good enough to sustain plant life within the confines of a container. Spread used container mix in your garden; and if you don't have a garden, give your excess container soil to a friend who does.

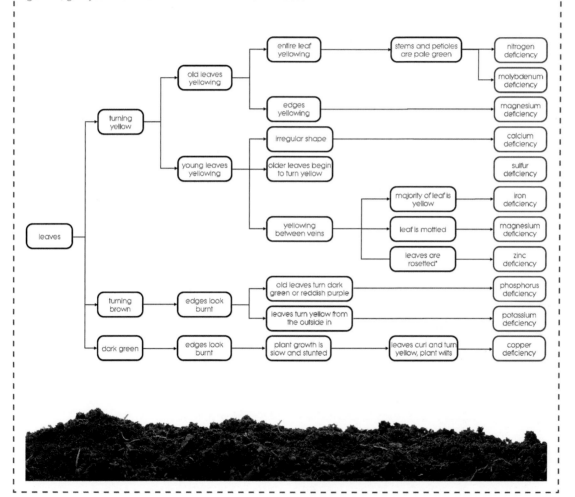

External Factors

Wind and sunlight availability are both external factors unique to the balcony gardening experience. Balconies that are higher up will experience more wind and, depending on the placement of surrounding buildings, may receive more sun. High winds + sun = dry soil. And there are a few ways you can combat these challenges.

1. Consider using a Pothole and WaterWick at the bottom of your pot. These not only keep soil from escaping out the drainage hole, they also hold onto water.
2. Mix coir into your soil blend. Coir is a coconut by-product and has the ability to retain up to eight times its weight in moisture. More water retention makes for happy plants.
3. Use porous containers. Clay and wood are porous containers — they breathe, allowing moisture to escape not only from drainage holes but through the material itself. I prefer porous containers to the alternatives, generally, but I use a larger-sized pot when using clay to compensate for the moisture loss. Use plastic containers if you find that you can't keep up with the loss of moisture.

4. Add mulch (straw or coir) to the surface of the soil around your plants to keep the sun from baking the soil and drawing moisture away from the plant.
5. Use a self-watering container. These containers are specifically designed so that you don't have to water as often. They contain a "holding tank" at the base and some contain a "wick" to allow water to be consistently drawn into the soil.

On the flip side, low amounts of sunlight can be a problem for balconies that are blocked by taller buildings or that face north. If this describes your situation, give the plants listed below a try. Minimal light, maximum harvest!

SHADE-TOLERANT CROPS	
Shade-Tolerant Crop	Sunlight Hours Required
Arugula	3
Bok choy/pak choi, komatsuna, tatsoi	2
Swiss chard (for baby leaves)	3
Chives	3
Herbs (oregano, parsley, mint, cilantro)	3
Kale	3
Mesclun	2
Mustard greens	3
Spinach	3

↑ A "pot hole" for drainage and "water wicks" to retain moisture.

THE ROOFTOP GARDEN

You could say that rooftop gardens are the "new frontier" of vegetable gardening: a space that is often overlooked but one that takes up significant area, especially in our cities. The roofs of buildings receive plenty of sunlight and clean rainwater. Like balcony gardens, though, wind and weight can be restricting factors. **Always determine how much weight can be put onto a roof before starting your project.**

Rooftop gardening is essentially the same as for the balcony garden. For most individual projects, you will use pots. For larger, community-based projects, raised beds may be installed on roofs that are designed to hold the weight. These projects require the help of professionals, however, and unless you are one, I would stick with containers.

The practice of growing vegetables on a roof is no different than growing vegetables in any of the other situations we have already discussed. The biggest difference is accessibility. While you are free to venture onto your own patio, balcony, or into your yard whenever you so desire, the roofs of many buildings have restricted access.

Each municipality has different laws governing the use of a rooftop as a garden. Check with your local municipality before you begin; determine if there are additional factors you need to consider: buildings codes, safety features, height (as well as weight) restrictions, and anything else your municipality may need you to assess and have installed before rooftop access can become a regular habit.

↑ My firewood shed with sempervivum green roof.

The roof you choose, whether it is that of your own building or another, will not only need to be accessible but practical. If the only rooftop access is a vertical emergency ladder, you are going to have a difficult time getting the materials to their final location, transporting water, and carrying produce to your kitchen.

Access to water is essential. Growing "off the ground" exposes plants to excess winds and containers naturally dry out more quickly than an "at grade" garden will. A tap and hose are the best options, but are not always the most practical. Consider installing a rainwater collection system (similar to a rain barrel) to redirect freshly fallen water. This type of system puts inconsistent stress in one area of the roof (it is heavy when full, light when empty) and so load capacity of your system's location will need to be determined by a professional. If you have only one or two containers, carrying a two-litre pop bottle of water up the stairs every morning will just be some good old-fashioned exercise.

The scale of your garden will determine how much detail you will need to get into. Larger, more extensive gardens may require electricity, surveillance, a supply shed, and gardening tools. If it's just you and a few tomato plants up there, the tools you will need can likely be carried easily to the roof when you need them: pruners, a harvest basket, a watering jug.

The entire green roof/rooftop gardening topic is well beyond the scope of this book. It could, in fact, be a book all on its own … and it is, many times over. See the Resources section at the back of this book for several great guides to building your own rooftop garden.

There are many considerations that are unique to the rooftop garden that can make it more challenging than any of the other three urban garden types we have discussed here. But don't let that discourage you. It may be too much for you to do alone, but perhaps others in your building or in the area would be interested in helping out. After all, four hands are always better than two.

↑ Co-operative garden on the rooftop of 410 Richmond Street, Toronto.

What should you grow? Which varieties are most likely to work in your small space? How big should the pot be for that cucumber plant? This section will help you understand what's available to you as a homeowner and how to choose the right materials for your particular growing project.

I'll discuss seeds and plants, pots and containers, soil and fertilizer. I want you to feel confident before you walk into your garden retailer or start browsing through the online catalogues. This is doing your research before you make a purchase: the more you know beforehand, the easier your purchase will be.

Choosing the Right Plants

The right plants will depend partially on you and partially on the available sunlight in your planting area. Make a list of the crops you would like to grow, based solely on what you like to eat. If you're like me, you want to plant everything (except Brussels sprouts. Whoever said we could eat those anyway?), but when you're working with small spaces, you have to be a little picky. Don't worry; I will narrow it down in the next step.

From the crops you've listed, remove any that aren't compatible with your particular light situation. If you're unsure, refer to the table on pages 24–25. A good number of vegetable and fruit crops are listed, but if any of yours are not, go to markcullen.com and search my "library" to find out.

Once you've narrowed down your choices to a manageable list of veggies that will work well in your space, it is time to consider what you are going to plant and sow your veggies in. How big is your raised bed? How many pots and planters do you have room for on your patio? Will you use pots or just railing planters

for your balcony? Be reasonable — remember that you still want to enjoy this space as you did before. If it helps, make yourself a rough sketch so you'll have an idea of where everything will go. Refer to the table on pages 24–24 to determine how much growing space some of the most common vegetables will need.

Finally, keep in mind that pots and planters can be easily moved, so these features are not permanent. The raised bed is a bit trickier to move around, but it's not impossible.

The following table (pages 37–39) will give you some examples of great varieties for small spaces. When you are shopping for seeds, look for packages that say "great for containers" or names that contain the word *patio*. These varieties are often hybrids that have been developed to be smaller and more conducive to container life.

Note that new varieties are introduced each season. Here is a list of my current favourites:

BEST VARIETIES FOR CONTAINERS AND RAISED BEDS

Crop	Best Varieties for Containers	Best Varieties for Raised Beds	Notes
Carrot	'Adelaide F1' 'Yaya F1' 'Nantes Touchon' 'Thumbelina' 'Caracas Hybrid' 'Little Finger' 'Short 'N Sweet'	'Bilbo' 'Big Top' 'Atomic Red' 'Lunar White' 'Solar Yellow' 'Purple Haze' 'Crème De Lite'	Container varieties should be short and well-tapered; for a different look, try round carrots that grow no bigger than a golf ball. Raised-bed varieties can be longer, but keep in mind that they will grow best in the light, fluffy soil within the raised bed itself. Try multicoloured carrots for something different. Taste is important to consider, too. Some are quite spicy while others are very sweet. Plant what you like to eat.
Bean (bush)	'Gold Rush' 'Eureka' 'Tenderpick' 'Italian Rose' 'Amethyst Purple' 'Prevail' 'Royal Burgundy'		Bush beans will do well in a container at least 20 centimetres across. Look for varieties that say compact, dwarf, or upright, as these will need less space to grow. Harvest times vary, but I like to pick them from the vine when they are about the thickness of a pencil. Raised beds are better-suited to pole beans as they take up space vertically rather than horizontally.
Beets	'Moulin Rouge' 'Cylindra Formanova' 'Kestrel' 'Solo F1'	'Detroit Dark Red' 'Red Ball' 'Early Wonder' 'Red Ace F1'	The smallest varieties should be used for containers. Raised beds can handle larger varieties, but still consider choosing small varieties that don't grow larger than about seven centimetres across.
Broccoli	'Di Ciccio' 'Waltham 29' 'Raab Rapini' 'Munchkin'	'Summer Purple' 'Premium Crop F1' 'Purple Sprouting' 'Green Sprouting Calabrese'	Containers need to be large (holding about 12 litres of soil); look for dwarf varieties for both the container and raised bed. Choose varieties that are quick to produce and continue to produce once main stem has been cut. A very cold-tolerant crop.
Swiss chard		'Bright Lights' 'Ruby Red' 'Discovery' 'Silverbeet' 'Bright Yellow'	Swiss Chard does very well in containers at least 30 centimetres deep and 30 centimetres across. Put three to four plants in a container this size. Any variety will do well in the garden or the container. Use it to add a splash of colour and as a nutrient-packed vegetable.
Spinach	'Giant Nobel'	'Samich Hybrid Semi-Savoy' 'Hybrid 7' 'Bloomsdale Longstanding' 'Red Kitten' 'Whale'	Choose spreading varieties for containers and the non-spreading, vertical growing types for the raised bed or garden so as to take up less space. All varieties that are good for the garden will also do well in a container. Containers should be at least 15 centimetres deep.

Crop	Best Varieties for Containers	Best Varieties for Raised Beds	Notes
Cucumber	'Spacemaster' 'Patio Pickler' 'Fanfare' 'Arkansas Little Leaf'		Choose bush type cucumbers for large containers and small gardens. Grow vertically to further optimize space. Choose containers at least 25 centimetres deep.
Lettuce	'Tom Thumb' 'Mini Green Iceberg' 'Tango' 'Oakleaf'	'Jericho' 'Freckles' Mesclun mix 'Summertime'	Lettuce can grow in very small pots: 15 centimetres or more.
Onion	'Red Torpedo' Bunching varieties 'White Lisbon'	'Red Wethersfield' 'Buffalo' 'Sweet Sandwich Hybrid'	Onions do best when planted in groups. When planting in rows, plant at least two of them side-by-side. Containers should be 25 centimetres deep.
Peas	'Provence (Container Variety)' 'Sugar Sprint' 'Little SnapPea Crunch' 'Peas-in-a-pot' 'Little Marvel'	'Green Arrow' 'Easy Peasy' 'Thomas Laxton' 'Super Snappy' 'Early Frosty'	Choose bush type peas for containers and the tall-growing, vine type for gardens. Stake peas to improve yield and reduce disease problems. Capitalize on vertical space in small gardens with a trellis or wire fence. Choose containers that are at least 25 centimetres deep.
Radish	'Purple Plum' 'Salad Rose' 'Perfecto' 'Black Spanish Round' 'Watermelon'		Radishes are small vegetables and will grow in pots and gardens equally well. The varieties here provide a few different shapes and flavours. Containers can be small: 15 to 20 centimetres deep at minimum.
Tomato	'Baxter's Bush Cherry' 'Tumbling Tom Yellow Hybrid' 'Totem' 'Green Zebra'	'Celebrity Hybrid' 'Black Krim' 'Orange Slice'	Containers varieties should be compact but still produce lots of fruit. Garden varieties can be a little larger, but if your garden is very small, avoid tomatoes with a spreading habit. Use a spiral stake to support the plants and double your crop in the process. Experiment with new varieties for some added colour. Deep containers, 30 centimetres minimum.
Hot pepper	'Poblano' 'Mariachi' 'Devil's Tongue' 'Jalapeno Raam'	'Ristra Cayenne' 'Zavory' 'Caribbean Red'	Twenty-five-centimetre pots minimum for best results. Hot peppers like warm soil (think about where they come from). Provide full sun.
Sweet pepper	'Sweet Red Popper' 'Tweety' 'Cherry Stuffer'	'Sweet Sunset' 'California Wonder' 'Pinot Noir'	Unlike hot pepper plants, which need a relatively small amount of space, sweet peppers require room for their roots to sprawl out. Choose large containers if you plan to go that route, 25 centimetres deep minimum.

BEST VARIETIES FOR CONTAINERS AND RAISED BEDS

Crop	Best Varieties for Containers	Best Varieties for Raised Beds	Notes
Kale	'Lacinato' 'Dwarf Blue Curled' 'Red Russian'		Kale will grow well in containers and in the garden. They grow upright and can be planted closely together. Twenty-centimetre pots will yield good-sized plants.
Bean (pole)		'Kentucky Wonder' 'Purple Podded' 'Carminat'	Pole beans are best suited to the garden but can be grown in large pots with vertical support. Pots should be large and sturdy enough to support the tall plants.
Leek	'Hannibal' 'Blue Solaise' 'King Richard' 'Bandit'		The leek hasn't really been modified to provide container-specific varieties. However, leeks will grow well in containers at least 30 centimetres deep. Start leeks in small containers and transplant once about six inches tall. Fill 30-centimetre container with only 23 centimetres of soil. As plant grows, hill up soil around leek over the course of several weeks, adding no more than five centimetres of soil at a time. This will blanch the stems, creating the white/green contrast that leeks are known for.
Zucchini	'Golden Delight' 'Defender' 'Venus' 'Eight Ball' 'Cue Ball'		Zucchinis are large plants. For small gardens and containers, choose the compact varieties. Choose large pots, at least 30 centimetres deep — the larger the better for these spreading vines. Because the vines tend to break over the sides of the container, consider tipping the container slightly to allow the vines to flow freely out of the pot.

↑ A seedling grown in a biodegradable container can be planted out pot and all.

Choosing the Right Pots

One trip to the local garden centre is all it takes to realize that there is a plethora of selection when it comes to pots and planters. Some are right for the task at hand (remember, you are planting vegetables here) and some of them just don't work. The right pot provides function over aesthetics. The perfect pot provides both.

Plastic: inexpensive, lightweight pots that come in a variety of sizes, colours, and shapes; usually with drainage holes, but if not, drilling some isn't difficult; relatively short-lived, lasting a few years. Plastics are a good choice where kids are concerned as they don't have the same potential as ceramics and clay to break if dropped. *Note:* if using black plastic, keep pots in a shady area to avoid them overheating.

Ceramic and Clay: relatively expensive, heavy pots (depending on the size); from the plain Jane terra cotta to the immaculately decorated, the visual impact varies greatly; long-lasting if cared for properly, but are easy to break and chip.

Metal: price is highly variable based on the type of metal; can be plain or decorative; many rustic recycled options available; non-porous and usually don't contain drainage holes if using a recycled metal container; drainage holes can be easily drilled; if weight is an issue, look for lightweight metals and shapes that best suit the future resident (deep for tomatoes, wide for potatoes, etc.); can heat up quickly causing root damage if placed in full sun.

Wood: often used for larger planters, prices will vary greatly; can be made at home (always use preservative-free wood or wood that has only been treated with non-toxic chemicals); can provide good drainage but this will depend on how they

are built; longevity will depend on type of wood used and how it was treated; provides good insulation for roots. Cedar is naturally rot-resistant.

Styrofoam: lightweight and inexpensive; not particularly attractive but can be decorated to look nicer; undamaged food-grade Styrofoam should be used; drainage holes can be made easily; good insulator so roots don't overheat; can be sourced from grocery stores who may have to pay to have them taken away. I sometimes use Styrofoam as a liner in a wooden planter to cool and insulate it: needs less water as a result.

Recycled Plastic Grow Bags: inexpensive and practical for small spaces; excellent drainage; great for annual crops and for people who may be moving; may lean if soil is unevenly watered throughout.

Woven Baskets: not particularly well-suited to growing vegetables; often comes with plastic liner which will not allow for proper drainage; removing the liner will allow for too much drainage; materials may contain harmful chemicals meant to keep the metals from rusting or woven fibres from being damaged by the sun.

* Reusing large pots from purchased garden centre plants is an efficient option. I use a mild soap and cool water to scrub away any residue from the previous plant, add new soil, and I'm ready to go.

↑ I prefer clay pots to any other.

Choosing the Right Soil

The right soil for containers and raised beds is engineered for this purpose. Garden soil or triple mix doesn't work well at all as it is heavy and dense. Weed seeds and diseases are harbouring in the soil and waiting for the opportune moment to strike. The soil will not drain properly and may become compacted. The result is an unhappy root system and a sad-looking, unproductive plant.

Opt for a good-quality potting soil or vegetable mix that is suitable for using in pots. These mixes provide adequate moisture-holding properties but also allow for proper drainage. The number one reason for problems with container-grown plants is overwatering. Vegetables don't like to keep their feet wet and too much moisture impedes root growth as it pushes oxygen out and away.

A good-quality bagged soil has some weight to it. Lightweight products contain a high concentration of peat, which provides little to no nutritional value. However, when peat is mixed, in the proper ratio, with compost, clay, and humus, the result is a well-draining soil that won't compact easily and will provide exceptional nutrition for most vegetable plants. If I'm growing tomatoes in a container, I put extra compost in my Mark's Choice container mix, which adds much-needed natural nutrition and microbes. A heavy feeder, like a tomato, will benefit greatly from this addition.

You can also make your own soil mixture, and while this may be a little more work off the start, you may feel better knowing exactly what's feeding the plants that will eventually feed you. Like "the best" chocolate chip cookie recipe, homemade potting soil recipes are seemingly endless. I will provide my personal favourite here, but don't limit yourself to this one. If you find that some plants do well and others not so, try experimenting with different ingredients until you find what works. I'll provide you with the most commonly used ingredients and the purposes of each and you can add and subtract accordingly.

← TOP: "Coir" coconut bricks need to be soaked in water for 15 minutes before use. BOTTOM: Use a quality container mix or potting soil.

MARK'S FAVOURITE POTTING SOIL RECIPE

1 part worm castings

3 parts sharp sand

5 parts peat moss

1 part vermiculite

COMMON SOIL INGREDIENTS AND THEIR PURPOSES

Ingredient	What Is It?	What Is It Good For?
Sphagnum peat	Partially decomposed moss	Balances air and moisture levels
		Additive to clay soils to open them up and to sandy soils to bind them
Coir	Coconut husk; a by-product of the food industry	Provides ideal pH
		Retains moisture and can absorb many times its own weight in water
		Slow to decompose
		Balances air and moisture levels
Compost	Decomposed organic matter	Excellent nutrient levels to boost depleted soils
		Improves soil structure
		Balances air and moisture levels
		A host of beneficial organisms reside in compost, helping to break it down
Manure	Treated animal feces: usually cow, sheep, chicken, or duck	Packed with nutrients
		Retains moisture
		Can improve soil structure (of very sandy soils especially)
Bone meal	Ground animal bones	High in calcium and phosphorus
Lime	Ground limestone	Provides calcium and magnesium
		Changes soil pH (increases acidity)
		Works to prevent diseases by raising the soil pH
Blood meal	Powdered blood	Source of nitrogen
		Can change pH (increases acidity)

COMMON SOIL INGREDIENTS AND THEIR PURPOSES

Ingredient	What Is It?	What Is It Good For?
Topsoil	Soil that resides on the top few centimetres of the earth. Sometimes topsoil is quite deep, almost 30 centimetres.	Can be purchased in different soil textures that contain varying amounts of sand, silt, and clay, so can be tailored to your needs Lots of living organisms to promote healthy root systems
Sharp sand	Not beach sand! Sharp sand, or builder's sand, is ground quartz. Particles are fairly large.	Provides plenty of drainage due to the large particle size
Perlite	Those little Styrofoamy balls you see in potting soils. Made from volcanic glass.	Improves drainage Increases aeration Reduces soil compaction
Vermiculite	Silicates that have been heated to create tiny pellets	Long-lasting, will not decompose or get mouldy Increases aeration and drainage Good water retention Excellent storage medium for bulbs
Worm castings	Earthworm waste; generally found in commercial worm beds and vermicomposters	Improves aeration and drainage Excellent water retention Very high in nutrients Will not burn plants
Sulfur	Varying sizes of elemental sulfur	Alters pH of soil (increases acidity) "Slow release" — works over time as the sulfur is broken down by bacteria
Leafmould	Leaves that have been rotting for at least two years	Retains moisture Provides nutrients, including many trace elements Works well in conjunction with sharp sand for a good balance of water retention and good drainage

Choosing the Right Fertilizer

Buying fertilizer is like shopping for disposable diapers. When my wife, Mary, sent me to the store to buy a pack for our new baby, I was bewildered by the selection. Here, I clarify the options for you so that you are not dumbfounded by the experience when you get to your favourite garden retailer.

The purpose of fertilizer is to enhance the nutrient content in the soil. For large-scale farms, soils are constantly being worked and planted, and despite rotation cropping, soils often need an extra boost of nutrients to be fruitful. For home gardeners, fertilizers are used to help grow large, long-lasting blooms on their flowering plants, juicy tomatoes, and a thick, healthy lawn. Each of these plants requires a different fertilizer, though: one that is designed to target the growth of the flowers, fruit, or foliage.

The N-P-K ratio is what tells us how that particular fertilizer will function and which part of the plant it will support best. Each number in the three-digit analysis on every package of fertilizer sold in Canada represents a percentage. A 19-31-17 fertilizer has 19 percent nitrogen, 31 percent phosphorous, and 17 percent potassium. The numbers are always represented in the order of nitrogen (N), phosphorous (P), and potassium (K).

Nitrogen (N) promotes chlorophyll production. Chlorophyll, the green stuff in plants, is responsible for photosynthesis. More nitrogen means faster green growth. You will notice that spring lawn fertilizers are always higher in nitrogen to promote the quick spring green-up.

Phosphorous (P) is important for root development, boosts bloom size, and increases the flowering potential of the plant. Fertilizers designed for flowering plants have a high percentage of phosphorous.

Potassium (K), also known as potash, supports root development and general plant health (including protecting the plant against drought, disease, insect damage, and cold). It regulates water storage, transport and uptake, and even fruit-ripening, among many other much more complicated tasks. Fall lawn fertilizers and fertilizers designed specifically for tomatoes (or a tomato/vegetable mix) will be highest in potassium.

You may have noticed that these three percentages do not add up to 100 percent. They never do. The remaining ingredients include other important nutrients and minerals: iron, calcium, magnesium, and sulfur, for example, are often added to a tomato fertilizer; boron, copper, and iron may be added to an orchid fertilizer; and manganese and zinc may be added to a general, all-purpose fertilizer. The rest is filler to keep us from burning the plants or over-fertilizing; it also helps to spread out the fertilizer evenly so it gets to where it needs to be.

Synthetic vs. Organic

How to even begin this topic? It's a heavily debated concept and one that comes with controversy. Most people are not fence-sitters, so let's discuss the pros and cons of these two options.

The choice is ultimately up to you. I prefer to use organic fertilizers when I can. My lawn benefits from an application of spring and fall fertilizers — yes, the synthetic kind — but my tomatoes and peppers grow just fine with a combination of homemade compost and well-aged duck manure, and a sprinkling of some tomato- and pepper-specific organic fertilizer as the plant begins to bloom.

SYNTHETIC VS. ORGANIC FERTILIZERS

| SYNTHETIC | | ORGANIC | |
Pros	Cons	Pros	Cons
Relatively cheap compared to an organic equivalent	Production process is expensive, environmentally speaking, and often employs the use of non-renewable resources in its process	Made from natural materials that are generally renewable and sustainable	Usually more expensive than synthetic fertilizers; but, if making at home with household and yard waste, then virtually free
Have the option of slow-release or fast-acting depending on your specific needs	Concentrated and fast-acting but provides short-term benefits without improving soil quality over time	If using homemade compost, you are diverting 35 percent or more of your waste from landfill	Bulky, especially when using composted materials or manures
Not bulky; easy to store if you don't have a lot of space	Long-term use can alter soil pH, increase problems with salinization, and reduce fertility	Natural materials contribute to long-term soil health, promote proper drainage, good moisture/oxygen ratio, balanced pH, and reduced erosion	They aren't necessarily safer for the environment; leaching can cause groundwater contamination and soil chemistry imbalances
Can choose liquid, granular, powder, or pellet form	Chemicals used in synthetic fertilizers can be harmful to sensitive skin, causing burns or rashes; long-term use of certain forms can cause respiratory problems	Less concentrated and less likely to cause plant damage if too much is applied	Breaks down slowly, which can be a problem if rapid solution is required
Predictable results	If directions are not followed accurately, concentration can be too high, resulting in burnt roots, leaves, and stems	If using on food plants, peace-of-mind knowing that you're not eating plants grown with synthetic fertilizers	If growing indoors, manures and composts that are not fully decomposed may give off a bad odour

A Final Note

There is a wide selection available to you and it can seem overwhelming. From seeds to soil, you have hundreds of options and in the end it will be your decision. I suggest starting small, with one or two pots or one raised bed, then add more once you get the hang of it. I'm hoping that the information here has given you the confidence to walk into your garden retailer and walk out feeling good about your purchase.

Obtaining the materials for your vegetable garden is the second step after understanding your space and what you want to grow. Caring for your plants from seed to harvest is the next.

Before you get to harvest food from your garden or patio/balcony, you must grow them. In some cases this is easier said than done. "Damping off," for example, can cause your newly sprouted shoots to keel over almost as quickly as those little shoots appear. And if they make it to the flowering stage, you may be faced with a slew of hungry beetles looking for an easy meal.

I'm not going to say food gardening is easy, especially as you may be new to the experience. While food gardening does come with a fair share of challenges (like anything in life), growing your own food is exceptionally rewarding. The following pages will take you through the life of a small garden: how to start, what to look out for, and, of course, the harvesting process (the reward for all of your hard work).

← Cotyledons are the first "leaves."

A healthy September harvest … ↑

STARTING SEEDS

The seeds you buy will be grown in one of two ways.

Method 1: directly sown in the soil.
Method 2: start indoors.

Living in Canada, you know that we don't have the longest growing season, so plants that inherently take longer to mature will need a bit of extra time indoors before they can be placed outside. Even so, I recommend that you sow some seeds directly into the pots, raised bed, or veggie garden. These are the fast-germinating seeds that perform best "direct sown." But if the package says to start early indoors, I recommend that you do it. Unless you want green tomatoes in September …

Direct Sowing

Direct sowing is fairly straight-forward. Place the seeds into the soil using the depth and spacing parameters listed on the package. I often use an aluminum "planting stick" with pre-drilled holes in it. This handy tool makes the job of spacing your seeds very simple. I use the rigid edge to mark my rows before I sow them.

Some seeds need light to germinate, and if that's the case, you will simply sprinkle them over the top of the soil rather than burying them. If burying the seeds is recommended, place them into the hole, cover with soil, and press down firmly. Water well, but allow the soil to dry to the touch between applications of water.

WHAT IS A COTYLEDON

Within a plant's seed is an embryo. This embryo is made up of several parts, including the tissues for leaves, stems, and roots. And a cotyledon. Upon germination, a seed will send its cotyledon to the surface of the soil to begin the first stages of growth. The seed itself only has enough energy to support the cotyledons and so it is their responsibility to soak up the sun and create sugars for the seedling so that it may develop its first true leaves. Some seeds keep their cotyledons underground, sending their true leaves to the soil first. Seeds may have one or two cotyledons, being called monocots and dicots, respectively.

A planting stick simplifies the job of sowing seeds. →

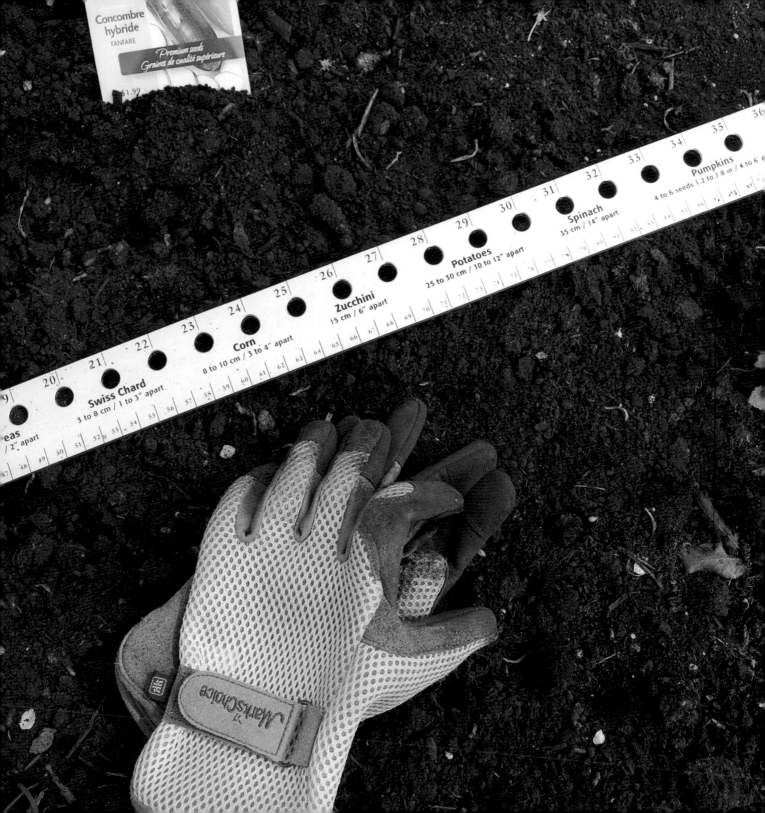

Starting Seeds Indoors

Starting seeds indoors requires a few extra supplies: shallow trays, egg cartons, small pots, and seed starting mix. Depending on how much light your sunniest window receives, you may also consider investing in a grow light, which is designed to produce UV light without emitting too much heat. Too little sunlight will produce leggy plants, that is, their stems are stretched trying to reach for more light. A grow light, especially in the low light conditions we Canadians receive in March and April, can be exceptionally helpful.

To make the process of starting seeds simple, I will lay out the instructions step by step.

Step 1: Using seed starting mix (not potting soil), fill as many small containers as you need to hold the plants you wish to grow. I like to use egg cartons, because they are free and they work as well as any other containers. For salad greens, I use plastic trays — the ones without the dividers. You can find these at garden centres and hardware stores as part of a seed-starting kit.

Step 2: Place one seed into each small container (or egg holder) and press down firmly with your thumb. For trays, I sprinkle the seeds across the width of the tray and cover either with the seed starting mix or a sand-based soil. Remember that some seeds need light to germinate. Be sure to read the back of each package for the specific growing method.

Step 3: Water well. Keeping seeds moist at this stage is important. To help retain moisture, cover trays with clear plastic (you can buy kits that come with lids, or you can use plastic wrap). I use a misting bottle to avoid washing the seeds away or causing them to congregate at one end of the tray.

Step 4: Once germination has occurred (that is, you see the cotyledon poking through the soil), remove the plastic cover and place the tray or egg carton in an area where it is sure to receive good air flow. For a few days I often prop the transparent top up to allow air to circulate around the young seedlings, eventually removing it all together. Watering properly at this stage is critical. Far too many seeds are lost every year to a disease called damping off. This disease, which can be avoided by not overwatering and providing ample air flow, results in withered and wilted seedlings.

Step 5: Water thoroughly with a misting bottle from the top, or pour water into a container to water from the bottom. Allow the surface of the soil to dry between waterings (frequency will

STEP 1

STEP 2

STEP 3

depend on the ambient temperature and the amount of air the seedlings receive).

Step 6: As your seedlings grow, the first true leaves will emerge. At this stage, if you have planted an individual seedling into a very small container, it will need to be moved into a larger container filled with potting soil. Seedlings in trays should grow a bit longer, as you will need to separate them from one another once they are a bit larger.

Step 7: Your seedlings will spend the next few weeks growing foliage and the roots will take up more space in the container. In time, your plants can start spending their days outdoors. They have been enjoying the warm hug of your house for several weeks at this stage so be aware that thrusting them into the hard conditions of external life will stress them. There is a gradual process, called **hardening off**, that will prepare the young plants for the harsh reality of outdoor life. Here are some steps to follow to ensure your seedlings have a smooth and healthy transition:

- On a warm day, approximately a week before you will plant them outdoors for good, water your plants well in the morning and place them outside in the shade. Leave them for half a day, then bring them back indoors.
- The following day, water them well and leave them in the shade for ¾ of a day.
- On the third day, water well and place the seedlings outdoors for the entire day, only bringing them indoors if the temperature will dip below 10°C overnight.
- By day four, your plants should be able to tolerate a bit of sun. Water well and leave them where they will receive the morning sun. Again, leave the plants out overnight if temperatures will be above 10°C.
- Leave your plants outdoors for the next three days, letting them dry out completely and even letting the plants wilt slightly. This will cause the roots to extend in search of water, ultimately creating more drought-tolerant plants.
- By the end of the seventh day, your plants will have been exposed to sun, heat stress, and wind. If temperatures are predicted to stay above freezing, the seedlings may be planted straight into your raised bed or garden or left in their pots outdoors. Make sure you choose an appropriate pot for the plant's final home, one that it will support its weight and hold enough soil to provide it with moisture and nutrients for the entire growing season.

STEP 4

STEP 5

STEP 6

Now That Your Plants Are Outside

Whether your plants will be spending their summer in the ground or in a pot, they will eventually all make it outdoors. Now that they are outside, they will be exposed to whatever Mother Nature decides to throw at them: wind, rain, cold snaps, droughts. For the most part, there isn't too much to worry about. I recommend staking tall plants (beans, tomatoes, peppers) to prevent them being blown over by the wind or pushed around by the rain. If it's early in the season, frost may still be a factor (as much as we would like to forget it by May), so in those early days,

listen to the forecast and cover any frost-tender plants overnight. I use burlap, laying it over the entire garden. Plastic bags work well to cover individual pots. I recommend that you water your plants in the morning to keep disease at bay and prepare the foliage for a day of hot sun. Many plant diseases require water to either transport from plant to plant or even leaf to leaf on the same plant. Water is also necessary for a number of fungal plant diseases to propagate. Watering in the morning not only keeps the plant hydrated, it allows the sun to evaporate excess water, drying out potential fungal problems.

GROWING INDOORS

In some of the harsher Canadian climates, growing all of your plants indoors is the only option. This small indoor garden was grown by a friend, Katie, while she lived in the Northwest Territories.

Using plastic milk jugs, she grew green peppers, tomatoes, jalapenos, and cherry peppers inside. Hand-pollinating all of the flowers resulted in a perfect harvest (and no bugs!).

One of Mother Nature's other contributions to your plant's life is a slew of insect pests and diseases. Of course, these organisms all have their place in the world, but ideally that place is not on your zucchini plant. Let's discuss a few of the more common problems we encounter in the veggie garden.

Bugs

I recently had a heated discussion about insects with a friend. This friend was so annoyed with the bites he received during a casual stroll through Algonquin Park, he stated blatantly, "Mosquitoes could just disappear and everyone would be happier for it! And you know what? Blackflies, ants, wasps, horseflies, and deerflies can just move along, as well, because they have no use!"

My jaw dropped. While I completely understand where he's coming from, I couldn't disagree more with his statement. Yes, these insects are annoying to us, and probably to many other mammals, but they are an integral part of the food web. These insects are food for birds, reptiles, amphibians, bats (who are mammals, by the way), and fish. If all of those insects disappeared today, we might be less itchy after a walk in the woods, but give it a couple of months, and we would start to see larger species drop off the map. Birds and bats would resort to eating important pollinating species and our food crops would be in a sorry state.

In the end, I didn't manage to convince him that his mosquito bites were for the greater good, but he did see where I was coming from. Within the food web, everything has a place. Most of the creatures in the web are food for something larger, more aggressive, or more cunning. As humans, we are at the outskirts of this web, along with other top predators; like them, our survival depends on the survival of the rest of the web. We are a part of an extensive ecosystem and we can't pick and choose who we want to live with. But we can pick and choose, to an extent, who we want to share our gardens with.

Ninety-nine percent of the bugs in your garden and those that come around to your patio and balcony are good. That is, they are pollinators or predators. And some of them are just there, not helping or harming.

That one percent, though, can be very destructive. And it can be frustrating to put all this work into growing and nurturing a plant, only to have it defoliated before it can produce any food. Here is a list of the top 10 most destructive insect pests and the best ways to combat them. Some of these are very host specific (the Colorado potato beetle is really only going to come around if you're growing potatoes); others are generalists (the Japanese beetle will defoliate almost anything).

1. Japanese Beetle

Eats: just about anything (known to be fond of more than 300 plant species)

Overwinters: in the soil, where it stays relatively moist during summer and fall (i.e., heavily watered lawns)

Damage Done: shotgun holes and skeletonized leaves; plant is left with no way to photosynthesize and annual plants will often succumb to this damage

Larvae: the white grub

Natural Predators: birds, parasitic wasps

What You Can Do: attract birds to your yard with feeders and nesting boxes; attract wasps with dill, cilantro, asters, and members of the mint family; avoid watering your lawn whenever you can

2. Earwig

Eats: living and dead plant matter; some will eat aphids and other soft-bodied insects

Overwinters: in the soil. In early spring, the female will lay her eggs and tend to the eggs and the hatched nymphs for about two weeks.

Damage Done: eats, in their entirety, the leaves and stems of young plants; skeletonizes leaves on older plants; will generally not touch mature plants; does most of its handiwork at night, as it prefers darkness.

Nymph: three to five instars (distinct life stages); takes approximately 50 days to reach maturity

Natural Predators: toads, birds

What You Can Do: attract toads with scrubby leaf matter and hidey-holes (they really like the rock garden at my place); attract birds with feeders and nesting boxes

3. Slugs and Snails

Eats: living and dead plant matter, flowers, fruit, and foliage of some tree species

Overwinters: in the top layers of the soil

Damage Done: irregular shaped holes in leaves, "chunks" missing from fruit

Larvae: no real larval stage: tiny slugs and snails are born from eggs; slugs take three to six months to reach maturity, snails up to two years; both begin feeding as soon as they are born

Natural Predators: birds, frogs, ground beetles, snakes, toads, turtles

What You Can Do: attract birds with feeders and nesting boxes; beetles with rocks or bricks they can burrow under; snakes and toads with scrubby leaf

↑ Japanese beetle.

↑ Earwig.

matter kept fairly dense to provide a cool place to lay; turtles and frogs need larger water bodies with plant matter surrounding and within

4. Cabbage Worms and Loopers

Eats: as its name suggests, enjoys cabbage leaves, but also kale, broccoli, and cauliflower (the Brassiceae family)

Overwinters: as pupae in the soil

Damage Done: begins as small holes in leaves, quickly develops into complete defoliation

Larvae: cabbage worms are the larvae of the cabbage butterfly, a white or yellow butterfly with six black spots on the inside of its wings; the cabbage looper is the larvae of a fairly innocuous brown moth

Natural Predators: yellow jacket and paper wasps, shield bugs, tachinid flies

What You Can Do: you'll not likely want to attract wasps to your garden, but tachinid flies are easily attracted with members of the carrot and parsley families, including carrot and parsley (obviously), Queen Anne's lace, dill, cilantro, and fennel

5. Colorado Potato Beetle

Eats: leaves of plants in the Solanaceae family, including potatoes, tomatoes, and eggplant

Overwinters: as adults in the soil. They burrow their way out of the soil in the spring and begin feeding as soon as host plants are available.

Damage Done: completely defoliates plants in a very short period of time if not kept under control

Larvae: a small brownish-red grub lined with black spots on either side of its body

Natural Predators: lacewings, soldier bugs, tachinid fly

What You Can Do: attract these insects with dill, fennel, and members of the Echinacea family. For heavy infestations, your best bet is to pick them off by hand, spray off plants with water, use an organic insecticidal soap, or install floating row covers.

6. Cucumber Beetle, Spotted and Striped

Eats: cucumber plants and other cucurbit crops such as squash and melon. Will eat leaves, flowers, and fruit. The striped cucumber beetle is most commonly found on cucumber plants, whereas the spotted cucumber beetle tends to enjoy other

↑ Garden slug.

↑ Cabbage worm.

members of the cucurbit family equally as much.

Overwinters: as adults, in areas protected from heavy snow — log piles, plant debris, and near homes where temperatures do not get quite as cold are preferred sites

Damage Done: leaves are first left with shotgun holes that quickly deteriorate to leaves that have been completely defoliated. Will eat the veins on younger leaves. Damage on fruit will appear as small surface holes or scrapes.

Larvae: small, thin white (or yellow) worms with brown or black heads and a brown or black spot on the back end

Natural Predators: soldier beetle, tachinid fly, and braconid wasp will prey on adults, lacewings and ladybugs will devour eggs

What You Can Do: attract these predators to your garden with dill, fennel, coreopsis, goldenrod, and native asters

Special Considerations: the cucumber beetle is a carrier of bacterial wilt. This fungus spreads quickly once a plant is infected and is characterized by leaves that wilt for no apparent reason. Once a plant is infected, you cannot save it, especially early in the

↑ Cutworm.

season. At the end of the season, you may still be able to salvage some of the fruit, but time is limited.

7. Cutworm

Eats: grass blades (lawns), seedlings

Overwinters: as eggs on grass blades or as eggs at the surface of the soil

Damage Done: very distinctive "sliced" stems. Grass blades and seedling stems will be cut at the soil surface or even just below it.

Larvae: the cutworm is the larvae of several brown moth species; characterized by their curling habit when disturbed

Natural Predators: tachinid fly, braconid, and other parasitic wasps

What You Can Do: attract these predators to your garden with dill, fennel, and other members of the carrot family. They prefer tiny flowers from which they feed on nectar and pollen.

8. Tomato Hornworm

Eats: tobacco and tomato plants; will sometimes eat pepper, potato, or eggplant

Overwinters: as a pupa, beneath the soil. Emerges in late spring as a moth.

Damage Done: will eat leaves and fruit, completely devouring both, and will take large chunks out of the larger tomato varieties

Larvae: the hornworm is the larvae of the sphinx moth, beautifully stunning moths that are often confused with hummingbirds. The larvae are large green caterpillars with white V markings down the sides and a large black horn at the back end. Tobacco hornworms look very similar, but the easiest difference to spot is the horn: tobacco hornworms have red horns.

Natural Predators: most notably, the braconid wasp, which lays its eggs inside the caterpillar.

Hatched larvae will eat the host's muscle tissue without killing it. If you have ever seen a parasitized hornworm, you'd know it: the caterpillar will have large silk cocoons hanging off it. These are the wasp larvae, which will emerge from the cocoons as adult wasps.

What You Can Do: attract braconid wasps with dill, fennel, and other members of the carrot family

9. Flea Beetle

Eats: almost any vegetable plant; will occasionally eat flower petals and leaves of non-vegetable plants, including trees

Overwinters: as adults in leaf litter, garden debris, or in areas that are sheltered from the autumn winds and rain

Damage Done: small shotgun holes in newly developing plants (vegetable seedlings are most often affected in my garden). Can damage the leaf so badly that the plant can no longer photosynthesize well enough to survive.

Larvae: very small (three to four millimetres) white grub-like creatures. They have darker heads and back ends. You will likely never see the larvae and, in fact, the larvae don't actually cause that much damage.

Natural Predators: toads, ground beetles, and small songbirds

What You Can Do: attract toads with scrubby leaf matter and hidey-holes (they really like the rock garden at my place); attract birds with feeders and nesting boxes; ground beetles like cool, dark places (under rocks, for example)

10. Squash Bug

Eats: winter squash and pumpkin

Overwinters: as adults in leaf and garden debris; particularly fond of plants that were previously infected

Damage Done: squash bugs (nymphs and adults) are sap suckers. They will use their piercing mouthparts to reach the liquids that flow through the plant's leaves and stems. Leaves will wilt and die. A serious infestation can quickly cause collapse of the entire plant. They will sometimes feed on immature plants, which will mature with surface scars or holes.

Nymph: early nymphs are pale green, looking similar to an aphid. They mature into the distinctive angular squash bug after passing through six instars (moults) during which they actually shed their exoskeleton to reveal a more mature insect each time. It takes about eight weeks to complete this process.

Natural Predators: tachinid flies

What You Can Do: attract with dill, fennel, and other members of the carrot family. Squash bugs do not have many natural predators and you would do best to use multiple methods of prevention and cure: choose resistant squash varieties; in early spring, when night temperatures still drop below zero, rustle up leaf and debris piles, search for egg masses in spring, pick off adults, install floating row covers.

↑ Flea beetle.

The Fungal Predators

Diseases can be equally frustrating to deal with. Unlike insects, diseases don't have natural predators or enemies you can lure into your garden to help. Many garden diseases that affect food crops are airborne, meaning you have no way of controlling their presence amongst your veggies. You can, however, take precautionary measures and recognize the symptoms of these diseases in an effort to keep the problem under control while your plants work to produce a harvest.

1. Powdery Mildew

Affected Plants: different species of powdery mildew will affect different plants. Commonly affected crops include: lettuce, grape, apple, pear, lilac, strawberry, tomato, zucchini, and other cucurbits (gourds).

General Description: a white or grey fuzzy-looking substance that settles most often on leaves and stems. The fungus does not generally cause the plant to die, but will cause added stress and weaken the plant, making it more susceptible to attacks from other diseases or insects, heat, or drought.

Prevention/Control: prevent powdery mildew by choosing resistant varieties of the plant you're looking for; apply an organic fungicide on susceptible plants; be sure to provide adequate light and air flow to the plant. Organic sprays containing sulfur have been shown to work well for prevention and control.

2. Early and Late Blight

Affected Plants: potato and tomato

General Description: early blight is characterized by brown or black lesions on stems, fruit, or leaves. The lesions develop a bull's-eye pattern of concentric circles. Leaves may turn yellow and fall off, stems can be girdled, and fruit will develop poorly or not develop at all. Late blight is characterized by black or brown lesions on the fruit, leaves, or stems. The spots look greasy or wet but

↑ Powdery mildew.

↑ Early blight.

can also appear fuzzy. Under the right conditions, late blight can consume the plant in a matter of days. Affected fruits will develop black sinkholes, or, if they are green, will develop large, circular brown lesions that appear to be under the skin.

Prevention/Cure: you cannot cure blight. Once your plant has the disease, it has it for its life and will likely leave traces of it in the soil. Your best bet is to prevent it all together. Every two weeks, starting on Fathers' Day weekend until the end of the season, spray your plant with a copper-based sulfur spray. When watering, do not get leaves wet (water at the soil level). And prune out branches to keep the air moving freely. Blight spores enjoy the hot, wet conditions that we generally experience at some point in our Canadian growing season.

3. Clubroot

Affected Plants: members of the Brassicaceae family, including cabbage, cauliflower, broccoli, radishes, and turnip

General Description: the plant aboveground is not affected until the disease has affected the roots. You will notice yellowing and wilting leaves. Belowground, the roots are "club-shaped" and swollen. Roots will start to decay and the plant will die. If the plant's roots are only mildly affected, you may not even notice the plant is in trouble, since the leaves will appear fine. Mild clubroot is characterized by slow growth and stocky roots.

Prevention/Cure: this may be obvious, but avoid buying affected plants or grow your own from seed (since the fungus is not seed-related). If clubroot has been a problem in your garden in the past, do not move soil from that area to another. The disease is carried in the soil. Affected gardens can be limed to increase their pH level, but it is always best to perform a soil test before going ahead with this. The pH should be higher than 7.2 to effectively control the spores. Where clubroot was a problem, do not plant affected species there again for at least two years after treatment has been applied. Unfortunately, once clubroot has set in, there is no cure.

4. Downy Mildew

Affected Plants: vine edibles (beans, peas, grapes, zucchini, cucumber), but many flower species are affected as well. Downy mildew is responsible for the wilting that occurs on impatiens.

General Description: unless you regularly and thoroughly inspect your plants, you will likely first notice the yellow spots or mottling on the top of leaves. The organisms first gather on the underside of leaves, giving the area a blue-grey tinge and causing the leaves to look fuzzy. Stunts growth and causes leaves to fall prematurely. Enjoys cool, moist conditions. Some species of downy mildew will survive only on living plant matter and is actually blown into Canada from the south in spring (the downy mildew affecting the cucurbit family is one example of this).

↑ Downy mildew.

Prevention/Cure: in the fall, clean up plant and leaf debris. Choose resistant plant varieties. When planting, ensure that circulation is adequate around susceptible plants; trim plants if necessary to create better air flow. Keep leaves dry (water at soil level) especially during the cool spring months. A copper-based spray is your best bet, organically speaking, for preventing and controlling downy mildew.

5. Mosaic Virus

Affected Plants: species of mosaic virus are specific to their plant host. Plants affected by mosaic virus include: beet, plum, tobacco, zucchini, squash, cucumber, beans, melons, potato.

General Description: the first symptom of the virus is the appearance of mottled leaves, giving them a mosaic look. It almost looks like a type of variegation, but the varying shades of yellow and green are raised and will appear like blisters. On some plants, leaves will curl, growth will be stunted, and the fruit that comes from the plant will be abnormally shaped. The virus can spread through insects, infected seeds and soil, and debris left nearby.

Prevention/Cure: there is no cure for mosaic virus. If your plant becomes infected, remove it altogether and dispose of in the garbage (do not compost). After handling affected plants, wash hands well and change clothes if there is a chance the plants came into contact with them. Resistant varieties are available for many susceptible food crops.

6. Rust

Affected Plants: each species of rust affects a different plant species. Wheat, apples, corn, onion, pear, garlic, hawthorn, rose, pine, poplar and fir trees, beans, hollyhock, snapdragon, and gooseberry are a few of the thousands of affected plants.

General Description: rust will most often appear as its name suggests: orange, red, or brown speckles. Sometimes it will appear black or even yellow. It often begins where the leaf attaches to the stem and spreads outwards to engulf the rest of the leaf. Spores are dispersed via wind, water, and insects. Plants will grow slowly and may appear stunted and, although rust doesn't usually kill the plant, it can negatively affect its ability to produce fruit. Prefers hot and humid conditions.

Prevention/Cure: choose resistant plants when possible. Avoid watering when conditions are right for spore dispersal (hot and humid) and keep watering to the soil only — the plant's leaves don't need to get wet. Check plants for signs of rust before you buy them, and, once a plant is home, give it enough space to promote good air flow. Clean up in the fall, remove leaf and plant debris if rust has historically been a problem. A copper-based sulfur fungicide can help control the fungus.

↑ Rust.

7. Bacterial Wilt

Affected Plants: members of the cucurbit family, with the exception of watermelon; a different species will affect tomato, as well, but is far less common

General Description: wilt does not cause exterior symptoms until about a week after the plant has contracted the disease. The inner workings of the plant are affected, causing blockages in its interior transport system. In other words, water can't move into the stem and leaves. Visual symptoms are easy to spot: leaf wilting that leads to wilting of the entire plant, for no apparent reason.

Prevention/Cure: like many of the other issues I've discussed here, there is no cure for bacterial wilt. If you are unsure if bacterial wilt is the culprit for your plant's death, cut the stem at soil level. Slowly pull apart the two pieces and watch between: bacterial wilt will cause a thick, sticky, sap-like substance to form within the stem and it will form a string of the stuff as you pull away, like melted mozzarella on a hot pizza. The disease is spread most efficiently by beetles (see cucumber beetles in previous section), so it is best to control those first. Remove heavily affected plants and dispose of them in the garbage (do not compost). Choose varieties that are less susceptible to the disease.

8. Damping-Off

Affected Plants: almost all vegetable seedlings

General Description: damping-off is not one singular organism. If you grow your own vegetables from seed, you will have probably seen the results of the damping-off condition, but other species will produce invisible symptoms. Seeds will germinate and, while they are still quite small, will just keel over and die. The tip of the seedling will be withered and the stem will appear to have shrivelled up and may be girdled. Oftentimes, if many seedlings are grown together, the disease will affect plants in a circular pattern. Some species of the fungus cause seeds to not germinate at all.

Prevention/Cure: use clean tools and pots to germinate seeds; this includes using soil from a trusted manufacturer. Soil should drain well and air flow must be good: the fungus prefers cool, damp conditions. And now for the lecture on watering. Most often, damping-off can be avoided with one simple step: don't coddle your seedlings. Don't water them every single day and don't let them sit in water. Remember, they are small, they don't need much water to survive, and any water they do need is needed by the roots, and you are trying to encourage them to grow downward anyway. Always water from the bottom or inject it into the soil so it doesn't sit on the surface. Allow plants to soak up water for no more than 15 minutes. If you are really worried about damping-off, you may also sterilize your soil in the microwave or oven.

9. Scab

Affected Plants: potato, apple, cucumber, peach

General Description: while not a common problem in the vegetable garden, it is one of the biggest concerns for apple trees. Scab will begin as a grey, brown, or olive-green fuzzy-looking spot on leaves (the underside is affected first). Over time, these develop into lesions on leaves and eventually fruit when it emerges. Secondary infections occur during heavy winds or rainfall when the spores from the primary infection are transferred to other parts of the tree. Affected fruit is edible but unattractive: it will contain black, fuzzy-looking lesions that may crack.

Prevention/Cure: there is no cure for scab. The best preventative method is to keep watering to the soil level. For scab on apple trees, I recommend a strict regimen of fungicidal spray throughout the growing season. I use a copper-based sulfur spray on my trees. Susceptibility varies between tree species, with some being completely resistant. If you'd prefer to avoid the mess of scab on your apples, choose resistant varieties that will grow well in your area. For potato and cucumber, remove affected leaves and monitor the plant. Although it will not generally kill the plant, it may open up the plant to other diseases.

10. Blossom End Rot

Affected Plants: tomatoes, peppers, melons, eggplant

General Description: not technically a fungus, but it can look a lot like one. On tomato plants, especially, you will notice that the fruit will develop a dark circular lesion on the bottom. The lesion will appear sunken and will often develop moulds on the spot. Because the problem is plant specific, based on calcium levels in the soil, it will not spread from plant to plant.

Prevention/Cure: this one is fairly easy to prevent (again, no cure). Ensure there is adequate calcium in the soil before planting your seedling. I crush up the shell of two eggs and place it into the holes before putting the plant in the ground. Bone meal will work the same way. This ensures that calcium is available right from the beginning. You can also add a fertilizer specifically made for susceptible plants, but avoid the addition of too much nitrogen, which can actually cause your plant to have trouble absorbing the calcium. Mulch around susceptible plants to keep water levels even.

↑ Scab.

↑ Blossom end rot.

Other Predators

Squirrels, rabbits, chipmunks, moles. These hungry critters will steal fruit from the vine, dig roots from the soil, and create tunnels that hinder proper plant growth.

Deter most of them by planting up a few pots with marigolds, geraniums, and lavender. Oregano, sage, and mint will also work and can double as a food crop should you be so inclined. Voles and moles can be "taken care of" with a lightly chewed piece of Juicy Fruit (the stick, not the chiclet) put into the hole. I also like to pop the tops off marigolds as their blooms are starting to fade and stuff them into the holes made by burrowing animals. The two methods work in opposite ways: the gum attracts the critters, they eat it, and have a hard time getting rid of it; the marigolds and other flowers I listed offer a scent that is not appreciated by these critters and they will find somewhere else to burrow.

Your other option is to provide them with food AWAY from your desirable plants. Provide something better than what your garden offers:

peanuts, for example, are usually a hit. Make it easily accessible and consider putting cages around your desirable plants at the same time, making them less accessible.

Finally, if rodents are persistent and nothing seems to be keeping them away, try a repellent. There are mixed reviews about natural repellents (human hair, blood meal, Irish Spring soap). Some will say their concoctions are foolproof, but when others attempt the same recipe, it almost seems to attract the very same critters it was meant to deter. The truth is, rodents (and deer) are different from one location to the next. They will have developed tastes for certain plants based on what's available, so egg-based repellents will work for some people and pepper-based repellents for others. If you are having a problem with animals destroying your garden or vegetable plants, experiment with different recipes (hundreds of which can be found online). It may be worth your time, too, to ask at your local garden centre. They may have some location specific suggestions.

↑ Plastic cages help to protect tomato plants from critters.

↑ Rodent damage.

HARVESTING: THE BIG DAY

It's the moment every vegetable gardener waits for: the first ripe tomato, brilliant orange (or purple) carrot, or shiny green pepper, ready for the picking. Most of this part is easy as pie, but there are a few things to remember.

Use the seed packages and the date you planted to give you a good idea of when the goods should be ready. These are just an estimation based on average temperatures, but they will certainly set you on the right track. Every crop is different when it comes to harvesting. Some can be left and they will remain unchanged for several weeks, while others will bolt, grow far too large, or become chalky and flavourless. The table on pages 66–69 is a simple guide to harvesting the vegetables we've been working with throughout this chapter. You will notice that I have given some large ranges under the "What the Package Says" column and there's good reason for that: fast-growing varieties are available (resulting in the shorter time). The growing season in most of Canada is short compared to the warmer climates south of here, and fall and spring are unpredictable, with cold snaps and frosts a definite possibility during these months. Choose crops that have fewer days to maturity to ensure success.

Storing Your Haul

After picking, digging, and snapping your produce from its former home, unless you plan to eat it all right away, you will need to store it for a period of time. I recommend picking only what you will use in the next few days, but sometimes you must pick something before it bolts. Lettuce, spinach, radishes, and beets come to mind, and often you're left with more than you can reasonably eat in a day.

Many veggies prefer the cold, moist environment found in your refrigerator's crisper, but some do not. Remember, too, that many fruits and vegetables expel ethylene gas that will speed up the ripening and decomposition of other fruits and vegetables. The list below will give you a better idea of what foods shouldn't be stored with others. It's always a good idea to keep ethylene-producing foods away from ethylene-sensitive ones.

For produce that will stay fresh longer, avoid damaging the skin. Damaged fruits and veggies are susceptible to rot and moulds. If you do happen to damage something during the harvest, plan to use it that day. Alternatively, you can freeze many vegetables successfully to keep them for a later time.

DEALING WITH ETHYLENE

Ethylene-producing foods

apples, apricots, avocados, bananas (ripe), blueberries, cantaloupe, cherimoyas, cranberries, figs, green onions, guavas, grapes, honeydew, kiwifruit, mangoes, mushrooms, nectarines, papayas, passion fruit, peaches, pears, persimmons, plantains, plums, potatoes, prunes, quince, tomatoes

Ethylene sensitive foods

asparagus, bananas (unripe), blackberries, broccoli, Brussels sprouts, cabbage, carrots, cauliflower, chard, cucumbers, eggplant, endive, garlic, green beans, kale, leafy greens, leeks, lettuce, nectarines, okra, onions, parsley, peaches, peas, peppers, raspberries, spinach, squash, strawberries, sweet potatoes, watercress, watermelon, yams

Bolted lettuce. →

Crop	How Long Until Harvest: What the Package Says	What to Look For	How to Store
Beans (bush)	54 days	Harvest when the beans are about the size of a pencil. Beans that are allowed to grow too large will become chalky and lose their flavour.	Wash only once you are ready to use them. Brush off dirt and put in the crisper. Rinse in cold water and only cut right before use.
Beans (pole)	65 days	Same as bush beans. Harvest when about the size of a pencil or slightly larger if you prefer. Yellow and green beans will become chalky if left to grow too large.	From the garden to the fridge. Don't wash them until ready to use. Store in a plastic bag. Blanch and freeze for storage up to 10 months.
Beets	50–70 days	Harvest before the plant flowers to retain maximum flavour. The package should say how large that variety will grow. Dust off the soil to expose the top of the beet and estimate its diameter. Pull when it has reached the right size.	Store in refrigerator with greens left intact if planning to use within two weeks. Can be stored in dry sand in a cool (1°–4°C), dry place if planning to store for longer. Only uninjured beets should be stored this way.
Broccoli	45 days	Cut off the main head before it flowers. Side shoots will likely grow; cut them off when they are a size you can use.	Can be stored two to three days in the crisper after heads have been misted and wrapped in damp paper towels.
Carrot	75 days	As carrots mature, their orange tops may push through the soil surface, causing them to turn green. Stick to the guidelines with this one and pick them when they are a size you are happy with. About two centimetres across the top is a general guideline.	Cut off green foliage, leaving a few centimetres. Dry in sun for a day (bring them in at night to avoid critters stealing them). Brush off dirt but put them in the fridge unwashed. Wash when you are ready to use.
Cucumber	65 days	Harvest continually when the cucumbers are a size you will eat. Look at the package to see how large they should get. Continual harvesting will keep more cucumbers coming.	Refrigerate immediately after cutting off the vine. Chilled cucumbers will stay firm for up to five days. They are prone to rot, so rotate them and remove excess moisture by wrapping them in paper towel before putting them in the fridge.
Head lettuce	70 days	Cut mature plant at soil level. Mature plant size will depend on variety so be sure to check the package.	Remove excess moisture by lying on a paper towel for 15 minutes. Store full head of lettuce, unwashed, in plastic bag lined with paper towel until ready to use. Will remain crisp for about seven days.

HARVEST AND STORAGE OF VEGETABLE CROPS

Crop	How Long Until Harvest: What the Package Says	What to Look For	How to Store
Hot pepper	95 days	The colour of a hot pepper will tell you when it's ready. Hot banana peppers are yellow-green; devil's tongue are bright yellow; cayenne are red, and so on. Know what colour your hot pepper should be and pick it when it's there. Hot peppers that are a lighter colour will continue to change colours. I have grown hot banana peppers that could have been picked when yellow but I left them and picked when they were orange and red.	Hot peppers can be used right away or they will store in the crisper for about a week without going soggy. For long-term storage, freeze them in sealable bags made for freezer storage or dry them. Use a dehydrator for quick results, hang them, or lay on racks. The humid Canadian climate can lend itself to mouldy peppers, though, so keep an eye on them.
Kale	55 days	Ready when leaves are about 20 centimetres long. Pick continuously throughout the season. Harvest from the outside and avoid breaking off the centre leaves.	Kale tastes best fresh from the garden. For short-term storage, wash leaves, de-stem if you wish, dry, and place on a paper towel. Wrap up the lot and store in the crisper for seven to 10 days.
Leeks	60–120 days	Pull when stalks are about 2.5 centimetres in diameter. Use a spade or fork if soils are compacted or heavy clay. Consider planting a few every week or use varieties that mature at different times to ensure a continuous supply of fresh leeks.	If not eating fresh, leave in ground to overwinter. Hill up about 15 centimetres of soil and cover that with several centimetres of straw. Or, harvest your leeks and replant them in a bucket filled with clean sand or peat that has been slightly dampened. Store in a cool, dark place. Leeks will go dormant. Add moisture periodically.
Lettuce (leaf)	40 days	Harvest leaves the day you want them. Can be stored for a few days in the fridge. Do not allow to flower, and pick leaves from the bottom up (or inside out depending on the variety), keeping some to continue photosynthesis.	Wash leaves thoroughly with cold water. Use a spinner or paper towel to dry leaves. Put dry leaves into a sealable bag and push out excess air before sealing. Stores well for up to eight days.

HARVEST AND STORAGE OF VEGETABLE CROPS

Crop	How Long Until Harvest: What the Package Says	What to Look For	How to Store
Onion	Bunching onion: 60–110 days Bulb onion: 80–150 days	Pull bunching onions when they are a size you desire. For bulb onions, wait until the tops have fallen over and then wait another 10 days for the onion to completely mature. Dig out with a trowel or pull straight up.	Bunching onions: rinse immediately after pulling. Blot dry with paper towel and store in sealable bags. Will store for a month this way. Bulb onions: lay onions out to cure. Mild onions should be used up within two weeks; strong onions should cure for up to four weeks. Cure in a warm, dry place with some wind but no direct sunlight.
Peanut	130 days	Wait until the leaves begin to turn yellow (this will be a good way into fall, most likely). Check one pod for its maturity — the pods should be a good size and the seeds inside should take up the interior space of the pod.	Unshelled peanuts can be kept in the refrigerator for about nine months; shelled peanuts, three months. Freeze for long-term storage.
Peas	60 days	Appearance will depend on variety. Snap peas should be harvested after peas are the size of a regular green pea. Snow peas are flat pods that have very tiny peas inside. Harvest both when pod is a medium size to avoid them growing too large and becoming chalky.	Do not wash or shell. Pick and place into sealable bag. Shell (if you want) and wash right before use. Will store this way for five days. To freeze: shell peas, wash well, and blanch. Drain and package for freezing.
Potato	50–120 days	For potatoes to eat quickly (within a few weeks), dig up when the flowers fall off; for potatoes to store over longer periods of time (months), wait until the tops have dried up.	If not eating right away, or within a few weeks, you will need to cure the potatoes to thicken the skin and allow for longer storage. Clean dirt off potatoes but never get them wet before use. To cure, place in a warm, humid location for 10 days. Place in a cardboard box with ventilation holes in the sides, discarding any damaged potatoes, which will only cause others to rot. Eliminate any light and keep cool. Store for several months.
Radish	21–45 days	Do not allow to flower. Harvest when top of radish has reached size specified on package. Radishes are very fast-growing vegetables, some only taking three weeks. Sow a few seeds every week for a continuous harvest.	Remove leaves and stems and wash well. Rinse in cold water; do not leave out to dry. Line a sealable bag with a paper towel and drop in the wet radishes. Add more paper towel if you have more than a few radishes. Refrigerates well for at least a week.

HARVEST AND STORAGE OF VEGETABLE CROPS

Crop	How Long Until Harvest: What the Package Says	What to Look For	How to Store
Spinach	45 days	Pick leaves from main stem as plant grows and you want spinach. Immature leaves tend to be less bitter. Do not allow to flower.	Pick and eat right away. Spinach can be stored in the refrigerator for up to three weeks. Do not wash after picking; dry leaves with paper towel and store in an air-tight plastic bag lined with a paper towel. For freezing: blanch, chill in ice water, drain, and package for freezing.
Sweet pepper	70 days	Harvest when you are happy with the size and colour. If you planted sweet yellow peppers, they will start green and turn yellow over time.	Best to eat these up as you pick them. Brush off any dirt but do not wash until ready to eat. Store in the refrigerator for up to seven days.
Sweet potato	90 days	Sweet potatoes don't stop growing until they're out of the ground or the ground freezes. Keep an eye on the calendar and check at the 90-day mark. If you want larger sweet potatoes, wait longer.	Sweet potatoes are best eaten after about six weeks of curing. After picking, brush off dirt clumps and store in a warm (26°C), humid place for eight days. Follow that by storing them in a cool (12°C), dry place for six weeks. Store for several months.
Swiss chard	50–60 days	Harvest the leaves when you want chard. Immature and mature leaves can be eaten.	Can be stored for up to five days in the refrigerator. For large bunches that you cannot eat within five days, blanch and freeze.
Tomato	Cherry: 70 days Moneymaker: 75 days Plum: 75 days Roma: 75 days	Harvest when tomato is red (or has a firm but not hard texture). Some tomatoes will never turn red (they are yellow, brown, purple, or green when ripe, so it's always good to know your variety). If tomato is almost ripe and a large amount of rain is forecasted, pick the tomato to avoid it splitting from the excess water. Place not-quite-ripe tomatoes in a warm, sunny window and they will ripen.	Do not refrigerate freshly picked tomatoes. Pick and use within three days. If you have picked unripe tomatoes, let sit on windowsill. Remove dirt with a damp cloth but dry well before letting them sit on the counter.
Zucchini	50 days	Zucchini are another vegetable that shouldn't be left to get too large. If left on the vine, they will grow to monstrous sizes. Pick when they are about 15 centimetres long and have the proper colouring.	Store in a sealable bag in the crisper. Will stay fresh for five days. Do not wash until ready to use. For long-term storage, cube, blanch, then freeze in sealable containers. Stores for about a year.

✿ FINAL WORDS

From seed to table, I hope this chapter has helped you realize that growing your own food is not difficult. The experience of growing your own food provides satisfaction, and, as I have discovered through my own experience, it becomes less work with each season. Having tended my own vegetable garden for many years, I do not see it as a chore. I look forward to the spring melt that reveals soil recharged with water, and I am inspired to undertake this season's plan. The compost spreading, seedling planting, weed hoeing, more weed hoeing, and the continuous checking for any of the bugs I listed in this chapter have become routine events that I enjoy.

Each year, I am delighted to see how each crop progresses and I am keen to make observations about what worked well and what did not. I learn a little every year, and I think that's one of the greatest lessons to take away from this chapter. Learn something, improve your experience, and not only will your food taste better, you will continually feel more accomplished. And who doesn't need a pat on the back once in a while?

This year, I encourage you to start growing your own food. Even if it's one tomato or some mixed salad greens in a pot, it's a start. You may decide it's not for you, and that's okay, but more than likely you will reach the end of the growing season and say to yourself, "Well, that wasn't hard. I wish I had grown more."

You should now have a good understanding of your own space and I'm hoping I stirred up a few ideas in the creativity pot. Take your time and draw up a few sketches. Be patient. The best part about living in Canada is that we are blessed with four seasons, and whether summer is just getting started or coming to a close, it will stop by again next year.

If you're worried about your "brown thumb," don't be. Start with one plant: one living, breathing, food-producing plant. Choose a variety that is disease- and insect-resistant for best results. Once you have your foot in the door and a growing season under your belt, I guarantee you'll be more confident and wanting to expand your gardening horizons. Don't be afraid of failure — there is no failure in the garden, only composting opportunities.

WHAT KIND OF ZUCCHINI ARE YOU GROWING?

A few years back, I had a friend ask me where he went wrong with his zucchini. The plant seemed healthy enough, with a few minor mildew spots, but nothing out of the ordinary. The fruit, however, kept falling off the plant. And it wasn't just any fruit: it was odd, disc-shaped fruit. My friend, it turns out, had picked up a scallop zucchini. Known for their squatty shape, they are the perfect for stir-fries and eating whole. They are just as delicious as the kind we see in stores, and make great conversation starters at dinner. If you'd prefer the regular oblong zucchini, be sure to check the label carefully before you buy (that goes for seeds and plants).

↑ Scallop zucchini

GARDENING FOR
BIODIVERSITY

CHAPTER TWO

I was taught differently. The idea of a great-looking garden in the view of my father, a professional gardener in his own right, had little to do with my vision of a dream garden. My wife, Mary, and I were discussing the possibilities of moving to the country when I made the comment that creating my dream garden would be reason enough for me to make the move. "Well, it is a field of soy beans, so go nuts," she responded, in reference to the country escape just a few kilometres up the road from our suburban property, the place where we had raised our four children.

My father had a rather traditional view of beauty, where gardens were concerned: trimmed hedges, tamed evergreens (sometimes in the shape of animals), and a lot of 2,4D herbicide on the lawn to control the dandelions. Indeed, we live in a different time now, but over the years I have embraced the changes of this moving target that is a "beautiful" garden.

When I was planning my 10-acre garden in 2005, I made it a priority to seek out plants that would attract hummingbirds, songbirds, and butterflies. Other pollinators would simply follow, as my criteria for plant selection did not exclude the bees or myriad other pollinating insects. I mix native and non-native species in my garden with the hopes of attracting a wide variety of creatures. There's room for both. The native plants not only look fantastic, they are where I see most of the pollinators and other beneficial insects. The native insects that have evolved relationships with these plants over thousands of years enjoy the blooms on my Echinacea (purple coneflower) plants and the late-summer blanketflowers.

The non-native species in my garden are no slouches, either. I will often see bumblebees foraging through the many dahlias from early August through to late frost. The lady beetles (native and non) find a good meal on my roses, making short work of the aphids that collect on the new growth. There are thousands of these intricate interactions taking place in my garden thanks to the combination of native and non-native plant species. While there are purists out there who will plant nothing but natives, I am of the opinion that if a plant attracts pollinators to my garden, it is worth considering.

The truth is, though, that the single most effective arrow you have in your quiver where attracting pollinators to your garden is concerned is water. Adding a water feature to your garden brings life in a variety of forms that would otherwise not exist there.

I support water-loving creatures with a small pond surrounded by grasses and blooming flowers that can tolerate wet conditions. The edges of the pond are sloped slightly and contain a number of natural rescue features for frogs and other creatures that may go into the pond and want back out, or

others who are born into the pond water but spend most of their adult life on land. The water is kept aerated with a great deal of plant life that both floats on top and sinks roots into the sandy bottom. The waterfall aerates the water and introduces oxygen, which helps to minimize the growth of algae.

I also keep an uncut meadow on three acres of my property. Standing in the middle of it, you will find many native wildflower and grass species, as well as several bird feeders and nesting boxes (27 of them, to be precise) of various kinds to attract, among others species, bluebirds, house sparrows, and tree swallows. I am still waiting for the bluebirds to nest in my boxes. I know they are around, as I have seen them across the road. If I've learned one thing, it is that housing birds requires patience.

There is a balance between the living and non-living things on this planet. It's hard to ignore just how important every creature is and how they are part of a web, not a chain, meaning that one creature is not just connected to one other, but to many others. No matter the size of your property or space, you can create wildlife habitat, even if it's just a few flowering plants to attract bees.

Chapter 2 is about just that: using your space to attract wildlife and support part of the complex web of diversity. We will explore plants that are great for attracting pollinators, how to put your garden to bed to support important overwintering insects, and why it's important to move away from the traditional manicured gardens we have become used to. Messy is good and you'll see why.

To my friends who still envision a great-looking garden using urban sensibilities of neatness and order, I remind them that the new Canadian garden is one that actually embraces rot and decay. More on that in this chapter.

← OPPOSITE; Echinacea (top left), dahlia (top right), and water lily (bottom).

← My pond — the single-best investment I have made in biodiversity in my yard.

BIODIVERSITY

Biodiversity is a relatively new word, an amalgamation of "biological" and "diversity," it has only been around for a few decades. Thanks to Raymond F. Dasmann, the term *biological diversity* made its first appearance in the late 1960s but didn't become a common phrase until Thomas Lovejoy introduced it to the world in a foreword written for the book *Biology: An Evolutionary-Ecological Perspective*. In 1988, E.O. Wilson popularized the term *Biodiversity* with the publication of his book of the same name.

Today, there are as many definitions of biodiversity as there are scientists who study the concept. And while there are no official definitions, a good number of them are complicated and wordy enough to seem official to someone. The Convention on Biological Diversity defines it as, "the variability among living organisms from all sources including inter alia, terrestrial, marine and other aquatic ecosystems and the ecological complexes of which they are part; this includes diversity within species, between species and of ecosystems."

Backyard Biodiversity

I think of biodiversity in terms of my backyard. Of course, biodiversity applies to each and every ecosystem that comprises this planet, but it's easier to think of it in smaller terms. My backyard is a conglomeration of trees, shrubs, small plants, insects, spiders, birds, reptiles, amphibians, and many other related organisms. I do not see all of them, and I doubt I ever will. The biodiversity that exists within my backyard is made up of all of these living organisms. If I plant a new species, say, something native like milkweed (*Asclepias* spp.), I have introduced a new species to the ecosystem,

thereby increasing the biodiversity of my backyard. Not only have I introduced a new plant, but there is a good chance that monarch butterflies will start to visit from a neighbouring property or the forested area nearby. Biodiversity is increased again.

The introduction of non-native species can go one of two ways. It either works in harmony with the native species, attracting native insects and increasing biodiversity, or it becomes invasive, taking over habitat previously occupied by native species. In the latter scenario, biodiversity can be decreased as the non-native species reduces the presence of other species in the area. If the non-native species does not provide suitable food for the insect community, diversity is further reduced as these insects either die off or move on to another habitat where food is more plentiful.

The Importance of Biodiversity

To be clear, diversity is important; it is essential to the survival of the entire system. In the agricultural world, a lack of diversity can be devastating: a single harmful organism can swoop in unseen and destroy the entire crop (the Irish Potato Famine is a classic example). Mixing species over a large area not only protects each crop from collective damage, but it increases the health of the plants (keeping in mind that some plants work well together and others don't). This is just one reason why farmers rotate their crops, growing a different species on a piece of land each year.

In a natural system, where humans are not purposefully placing plants for aesthetic appeal, you will notice that monocultures do not exist. A forest dominated by sugar maples will not contain exclusively this species. Beech, ash, basswood, and aspen will be mixed in and the understory species will vary considerably with the light, moisture, and

A monarch caterpillar enjoys milkweed in my garden. →

soil conditions. The forest ecosystem protects itself from complete destruction by integrating multiple species within. Ecosystems are a balancing act.

The species within an ecosystem work in harmony to create a system that functions and can withstand unpredictable forces (natural and unnatural). Some ecosystems have even evolved to work only with the presence of destruction. The boreal forests, those which cover more than half of our land mass, are no strangers to periodic fires. These fires, started spontaneously with the buildup of dry material and heat waves or lightning, provide numerous ecological services. In addition to controlling the spread of invasive weeds, the heat put off by a forest fire is necessary to open the cones of the Jack pine, which are sealed with a resin that can only be melted by intense heat. Other native species that have been part of the ecosystem for thousands of years are tolerant of fire and put down seeds that can withstand the heat.

Biodiversity in the City

It's no boreal forest, but the biodiversity that exists within urban environments is no less important than that which exists in rural or remote areas of the country. I believe it's even more important to support the non-human life that shares these spaces. Remember, they are only "urban" because we have built them up to be that way. Many of the species that lived here before we came along will have moved on and found new homes, especially those too large to occupy the remaining forest habitats. Some others have become extinct. But this does not mean we should ignore all of those who have stuck around.

In the next part of this chapter, I will discuss the diversity that Canadians are fortunate to experience and how it has changed with the emergence of large urban expanses. Keep in mind that the focus of this

← We can learn a lot from nature.

chapter is to help you understand biodiversity, and if you want to understand it, you can't embrace the good stuff while sweeping under the rug the news that is hard to hear. There are many ways in which you, even condo owners, can support wildlife and biodiversity in your community. Some of us just need a reason, and I'm here to give you one.

Biodiversity in Canada

Leave Canada and ask non-Canadians what they think of this great land and you will be inundated with words like *peaceful*, *beautiful*, and *vast*. You will, no doubt, hear them speak of the Rocky Mountains, maple trees, ancient forests, fjords, geese, moose, and the natural beauty. In asking a few people myself, I was even given the word *combine* — yes, the farm equipment, which speaks to the vast open prairies of Canada's West.

And while we do, indeed, have a beautiful country, one filled with boreal forest, five great lakes that contain 60 percent of the world's fresh water, and three exceptional ocean coasts, we are losing species left and right. Our urban centres are expanding in all directions and monoculture farmscapes are pushing up against them. Exotic species are moving in, taking over, and becoming aggressively invasive. *Biodiversity is decreasing.*

Here is a look at the various categories of living things that come together and create the biodiversity we have in Canada.

↑ The view of Vancouver from top of the hill at Queen Elizabeth Park.

Birds

Whether you are sitting on a park bench or waiting for a bus, spending some time in the open country or hiking some densely covered trails, birds are likely one of the first glimpses of wildlife you will see. Many of the birds that live in our urban centres are accustomed to human activity and will split their time between nesting and seeking out well-stocked feeders. Throughout Canada, we have more than 450 bird species that either spend their time here year-round or spend their spring and summers here mating, singing their little hearts out early in the morning, and raising their young.

All is not well in the bird community, however. According to a 2012 article, "The State of Canada's Birds," of the roughly 450 species native to this land, 66 are endangered, threatened, or of special concern due to their dwindling numbers. Close to 45 percent of sufficiently monitored species have shown a decrease in numbers, and as food sources, nesting areas, and habitat continue to be destroyed, I can only predict that number to increase.

Increases in numbers (specifically in the raptor, waterfowl, and colonial seabird populations) can be largely chalked up to human intervention. Reasons behind losses seen in grassland birds, aerial insectivores, and shorebirds vary as drastically as their habitat and food preferences.

↑ A cardinal adds a pop of colour to the winter landscape.

The decline of grassland bird population can be attributed largely to habitat loss or disturbance; pesticide use has impacted food sources for aerial insectivores like swallows, not only here in Canada, but in the southern areas where many overwinter; shorebirds migrate long distances each year and depend on certain stopovers to aid in their journeys, but many of these areas are being altered or destroyed.

Mammals

Conservation efforts for mammals in Canada are well-known among Canadians. Many of those being protected are what I would consider charismatic megafauna, or, the cute, cuddly-looking ones. This list includes the cougar, sea otter, beluga whale, caribou, and polar bear, among others.

They are endangered, threatened, or at risk in some other capacity. Their numbers are in decline and, much like the situation with the birds, the reasons vary, but most of the decreases can be attributed at least partially to habitat loss.

Amphibians

The wetter, water-loving cousins of the reptile family, amphibians, are not generally on our radar. For starters, they are small. They also prefer to stay where temperatures are cool and conditions are moist (under rotting logs, beneath rocks, between decomposing leaves), so they are not seen all that often unless you go looking for them. Salamanders, newts, frogs, toads, and the lesser-known caecilians are all members of the amphibian family. All of the species within this group breathe and absorb

↑ The eastern red-backed salamander and other amphibians are extremely vulnerable to environmental changes.

moisture through their skin, making them extremely vulnerable to environmental changes. Spending part of their life in water and part of it on land, they are exposed to pollution in ways that other creatures are not. For this reason, they are considered indicator species: their health is directly related to the health of the ecosystem in which they are living. Pollution and habitat loss are the largest factors in their decline.

Not far from my home, the Jefferson salamander, an endangered amphibian, is facing troubled times as developers continue to pursue the land where they live. The good news is that these development proposals are *usually* turned down, allowing the salamanders to continue living, unharmed.

In Burlington, Ontario, roads have even been closed during important Jefferson salamander migratory mating days to allow the creatures to safely cross the roads that tear through their habitat.

Reptiles

The snakes, lizards, and turtles of Canada have a hard time. So many people fear the scaly, dry-skinned creatures that killing them or removing preferred habitat in backyards is often not given a second thought. Conservationists are constantly reminding people to drive cautiously during mating season to reduce the risk of hitting road-crossing reptiles as they migrate to breeding grounds or to lay eggs. They are fiercely stubborn about where they complete various life stages and a roadway isn't going to stop them.

Insects and Spiders

Definitely the most diverse group here, insects, like reptiles, get a bad rap. Of course, some of them are quite destructive (those are usually the ones that have been introduced, like the emerald ash borer) and some of them can inflict a painful sting or bite. For the most part, however, we can live in harmony with the creepy crawlies. In fact, we need them and so does every other species on the planet. Being small and packed with protein, they are a necessary food item for thousands of birds, fish, reptiles, and even mammals (see bats). They pollinate plants eaten by herbivores and omnivores, including us. And they break down organic matter in a most efficient manner.

The widespread use of pesticides has been destructive to insect populations, some far more than others. Moths, butterflies, and anything that migrates are susceptible to habitat change or loss. Many are exposed to chemicals sprayed on farms throughout the U.S., Mexico, and Central America. The fate of the honey bee (not native but important to the agricultural industry) and native bees, of which there are more than 400 species, is particularly well-known as their numbers continue to diminish — a phenomenon attributed to neonicotinoids, various bacteria and viruses, or a combination of the two.

Millipedes like these work hard to aid in the decomposition of organic matter. ↑

FLORA

We might not think of plants as things that can be threatened, but like all of the animal species we just talked about, plants are susceptible to pollution, habitat loss, and pesticide use (only in the case of plants, it's herbicides). Pink coreopsis and eastern prickly pear cactus are just two of the many plant species protected under the SARA (Species at Risk Act) and a provincial Endangered Species Act. In fact, at the time of writing, 220 plant species were listed as being "at risk" in Canada.

Invasive species take over habitat just like human populations do and herbicides are applied to areas where we want another species to be growing (chiefly, this means some form of agricultural crop). We venture into natural areas and dig up plants or pick flowers, effectively removing them from their habitat, and while plants are made to take in carbon dioxide, they are being poisoned by the many harsh pollutants that we expel.

Trees and Shrubs

Canada is known, at least in part, for its trees. In asking my "outsider" friends (those who do not live in Canada) what they think of when they picture Canada, nearly all of them supplied me with an answer that had something to do with trees. Whether it was a specific species, "maple trees," or just speaking in generalities, "ancient forests," "forest habitats," or "the colours of autumn," it's clear that when people think of Canada, they think of trees.

In Canada, the cucumber tree, blue, white and black ash, hop tree, American chestnut, butternut, cherry birch, Kentucky coffee tree, red mulberry, felt-leaf willow, Turnor's willow, sweet pepperbush, and dwarf hackberry are at risk in some capacity.

Many of these species require unique habitats to survive and some have been harvested to such extremely low numbers that recovery is nearly impossible. Some species rely on a dense population for survival: the cherry birch, for example, is wind pollinated, requiring another species nearby to cross-pollinate and produce viable seeds. No trees in the vicinity means the pollen is being blown aimlessly through the air with no hope of finding a flower in need of pollination.

← Pink lady's slipper. Not endangered, but uncommon, it requires a special type of fungus in the soil to break open the seeds and grow. Its numbers are decreasing due to unsuccessful attempts to dig up the plants and move them into gardens. Without the fungus, however, the plant cannot survive.

← Kentucky coffee trees are a Carolinian species that produces a large, flat pod filled with seeds.

A big part of keeping our native species healthy is recognizing the invasive species that are causing harm. Hundreds of species are introduced from other countries every year, but they don't all become invasive. In fact, many gardens contain non-native species that stay right where they belong (which is what we want). In order for a non-native species to become invasive, it first must be able to survive when it lands here. It must then be able to reproduce and become established. If it reproduces slowly, its chances of survival are minimal, but if it produces thousands of viable seeds or lays hundreds of healthy eggs in a season, its chances of survival are greatly increased. Finally, it must be able to thrive in its surroundings: thriving in the sense that it can find food, handle the climate, and reproduce effectively with limited predators, diseases, or parasites to stop it.

Knowing which species in your area are invasive is an important step to controlling them. If you have a yard, no matter its size, learn the plants that exist there. Learn to recognize them in the spring when they are small, and if something new shows up, keep an eye on it and identify it as soon as you can. Remove it if it's listed on your regional invasive species list (see the Resource Guide in the back of this book for regional listings). Always understand how to remove an invasive plant before you go ripping into it — some plants are inherently dangerous to skin, eyes, and lungs. Giant hogweed, for example, secretes a chemical that causes burns to the skin when contact is made. Unfortunately for most people, the burns don't just go away after a time: areas where the chemical touched the skin become sun-sensitive and burns can reoccur years after the initial reaction. And if the chemical gets into the eye, blindness is a definite possibility. These aren't the types of things you want to be taking lightly.

Call a professional if you are not completely sure what you are doing. If you live in an apartment or condo, make frequent trips around the green spaces in your area. If you notice anything unusual, speak with the person or group in charge of the landscaping.

I am often asked why it's important to keep track of and manage invasive species. I get the classic, "But, they're just trying to survive. Why do we need to get involved?"

My response is always the same: in their native country, they are surviving. They are part of a larger ecosystem that has developed natural predators to keep them in check. Where no predators exist, we need to get involved because they have no enemies. We brought them here and we are responsible for any damage they may cause. Millions of dollars a year are invested in keeping non-native species out, controlling ones that have become established, and repairing the damage they have caused.

Invasive Plants

Invasive plants compete for light, nutrients, water, and space. Fast-growing, aggressive spreaders can cripple trees, shrubs, and other plants. Often invasive plants will spread using rhizomes (roots) rather than

Cow vetch is a common invasive species that strangles other plants. ↑

by seed. Rhizomatic plants are especially difficult to control as roots can continue to survive even when the plant has been cut down or pulled out. Invasive plants that spread by seed usually produce thousands of seeds in a very short period of time. The seeds, unlike many North American natives, don't need

winter to germinate and will grow into plants that will produce seeds in the first year.

Invasive Insects

Invasive insect damage is usually seen before the insect itself. The first sign of damage is usually defoliation, when the insect will eat extensive amounts of foliage, leaving the tree or plant looking bare. Gypsy moths and Japanese beetles are well-known for their defoliating habits. Without leaves, the tree cannot photosynthesize or produce sugars and will eventually die.

Insects that burrow beneath the bark and feed on internal structures will often interfere with the tree's ability to move water and nutrients from the roots to the leaves. The emerald ash borer works in this fashion. As I write this, the emerald ash borer is devastating the ash tree canopy in Ontario and Quebec and moving east, west, and north as it searches out new trees. Because damage is not visible right away, a tree has to be heavily compromised before we know enough to do something about it.

Finally, insects may not be the direct cause of damage, but a vector for a disease that cripples the tree. Dutch elm disease is spread by elm bark beetles that emerge from infected trees and carry fungal spores to healthy trees. Since the 1940s, when the disease made it to Canada, upwards of 80 percent of elm trees in eastern Canadian cities have been lost. Elm trees were often used as shade trees in front and backyards, and because the disease spreads so rapidly with the help of the beetles, it wasn't long before those trees were being replaced with something else. There are several thousand elm trees left in the eastern part of Canada: they have either been spared due to their distance from other elms or they were part of the lucky few to be immune to the disease. Either way, researchers are still working to

↑ TOP: Phragmites (an invasive species) spreads quickly and out-competes native plants. BOTTOM: Japanese beetle damage.

increase survival rates for the elm trees that are currently unaffected throughout Canada.

Here are ten of the most common invasive plants and insects to keep an eye out for in your garden and neighbourhood.

Invasive plants:

purple loosestrife
kudzu (ON)
dog-strangling vine (ON)
Himalayan blackberry (BC)
salt-cedar (prairies)
common reed (Phragmites) (ON, QC)
buckthorn
giant hogweed
garlic mustard
bird vetch/cow vetch

Invasive insects:

emerald ash borer
Japanese beetle
Asian long-horned beetle
brown marmorated stink bug
gypsy moth
lily leaf beetle
brown spruce longhorn beetle
balsam wooly adelgid
rusty tussock moth
common pine shoot beetle

Refer to the Resources section for an extensive guide to invasive alien species. Note that each province and territory in Canada has its own methodology of reporting invasive species.

I'm going to sneak in a word of warning here: **don't move firewood**. Not only does it come with hefty fines throughout the country, you also increase the potential for spreading invasive insects, plants, and disease. Visit the Canadian Food Inspection Agency website for more information on the limitations of moving firewood and the related consequences.

When I discuss the topic of biodiversity with most people, their natural inclination is to ask, "What can I do to make a positive difference?" I am delighted to report that there is much that we can do. Please read on!

TOP: The destructive Japanese beetle. BOTTOM: Gypsy moth caterpillars. ↑

⚜ INCREASING BIODIVERSITY

The most recent census information tells us that Canada's population was 80 percent urban (urban being defined as having at least 1,000 people per square kilometre). That's a huge percentage of us that live and garden in relatively small, urban spaces; but that shouldn't be a reason to ignore the need for biodiversity. Canada is known for its cultural diversity, why shouldn't this diversity extend beyond our own species?

It turns out that gardeners across the country are changing the way they garden. Gone are the days of the highly manicured, completely weed-free, water-every-day gardens. Today's gardeners are too busy and don't have endless hours to fuss over weeds. Canadian gardeners are seeking out plants that can grow with what nature provides, demanding less from the gardener and relying more on nature for nurture. For many, garden standards have dropped. I don't mean that gardens don't look as nice; I mean that where we once sprayed chemicals on aphids and mites, we now use more natural methods of attracting hungry predators; where high-maintenance exotic plants were once popular, native plants that are better able to manage on their own are the order of the day.

← The black-eyed Susans that grow along my driveway have self-sown on the gravelly edge. I have never planted them, but thanks to the birds distributing the seeds, they provide a burst of colour from June to September.

Our Vision Is Changing

The gardens of today (and if my prediction is correct, the future) are as visually stunning, just in a different way. Increasingly, native plants are coming into focus, not only for their looks but for their contributions to the garden ecosystem. A 2013 study out of Switzerland determined that people's perceptions of gardens in terms of aesthetics are positively correlated with their ecological value (i.e. more natural looks better). What was once considered messy or unkempt is now often seen as both beautiful and ecologically satisfying. I call it "managed chaos."

There is a line, though: a fine line between messy but attractive and messy but wild (wild being unattractive, according to the study). There are, of course, a number of factors at play in a study like this, but I think I can say with certainty that natural spaces are becoming more common as we begin to realize their importance to the environment. In fact, a 2007 U.S. study surveyed 126 home gardeners, and the majority said they gardened mostly to experience nature.

The 2013 Swiss study pointed out that while we are interested in either incorporating environmentally functional (or native) plants into our gardens and other spaces, or converting them completely, we don't know how. There are common misconceptions surrounding native plants that hinder their use in our gardens and on our balconies. Here is my response to the most popular objections to "'going native."

Growing native plants is difficult. It is true that using native plants is different, but I would not say that it is any more difficult than gardening with non-native plants. As gardeners become more interested in growing native plants, more garden centres make them available. I recommend that you choose native plants that have been grown locally for best results.

Growing native plants from seed is less difficult than you might think. Most native plants are best planted from seed in the fall before the snow hits. Think about it: that is what nature does. Because they're native (and existed long before the Europeans arrived here more than 500 years ago), they can handle the Canadian winters and long, hot summers we experience here.

The final word on growing native plants from seed is to treat them as you would any other seed. Plant them where you want them. Start them in pots (but instead of starting them indoors in February, start them in November and leave them outside all winter). The only difference between seeding cultivated plants vs. native plants is that they need winter to break down the seed coat if they are hardy perennials.

My space is too limited for native plants. A good number of native perennial wildflowers do, indeed, need deep soil to put down roots and grow successfully. The deep roots associated with so many native plants are a huge part of their success in our harsh climate. But they're not all like that. You will need fairly deep containers (about 30 centimetres [12 inches] minimum) — not unlike the ones you'd use for growing tomatoes.

I recommend that you try growing in containers the native plants listed in the table on page 93. Keep sunlight requirements in the back of your mind as you make your selection, and remember that there are a good number of native plants out there that will do well in full to part shade.

Won't native plants spread and take over?
While it's true that some native plants spread aggressively, keep in mind that many non-native plants do, too. Plants that spread with abandon are usually those that multiply by rhizomes rather than by seed (or a combination of the two). Because the main plant is already established, rhizomes do not need to struggle getting to that point. Choose your native plants carefully and understand how each of them reproduces before purchasing or planting. Opt for the less aggressive alternative if there is one: common milkweed (*Asclepias syriaca*), for example, an essential egg-laying habitat and food source for monarch butterflies, spreads by rhizomes. Where you see one the first year, you will see five new ones cropping up the next. The non-rhizomatic alternatives, red milkweed (*Asclepias incarnata*) or butterfly weed (*Asclepias tuberosa*), also feed monarchs and their larvae, but won't spread like the common variety.

You may also decide to keep aggressive plants in containers, which is a great alternative. Simply sink the containers into the soil and cover — no one is the wiser and the roots are contained and kept under control.

← Butterfly weed is a unique alternative to the rhizomatic common milkweed. Monarchs will lay their eggs on these plants and the nectar-producing flower provides food for a number of other insect species.

CHOOSING THE RIGHT PLANTS

Native Canadian wildflowers are the best choice for maximizing biodiversity and providing food and shelter for native species in your garden. Often, though, knowing what's native and what isn't can be tricky. To this end, I have suggested a few books in the resource guide that may help you decide which species are best for your particular space.

When deciding which plants to put where, there are a few elements you *must* factor in and a few that are optional:

1. Location

In containers: choose wildflowers with shallow roots or those that naturally grow in dry landscapes.

In the yard: choose non-spreading plants or those that don't spread aggressively.

For both growing situations, consider carefully the sunlight and soil when making plant selections. A good many wildflowers prefer full sun, but there are options for shade (something has to grow under the trees along the forest floor). When you read the information on a plant tag, it's good to know what they're talking about. In terms of sunlight, this is how I would break it down:

Light exposure

Full sun: 6+ hours of sun
Partial sun: 3–6 hours of sun
Shade: 0–3 hours of sun

Soil

Container soil is easier to control — choose one based on the type of plants you wish to grow. Some plants, sedums and sempervivums (such as hen and chicks), for example, prefer an open, gritty, sand-based soil, but most containerized plants perform well in a high-quality all-purpose mix, like Pro-Mix or my own Mark's Choice container mix.

The soil in your yard is not as easy to control and you will likely find it easier to choose plants based on your soil type than to change it dramatically to meet the needs of certain plants. Work with Mother Nature; don't fight her. Ditto for sunlight.

NATIVE PLANTS AND THEIR REQUIREMENTS

Common Name	Latin Name	Sunlight Requirements	Soil Requirements
Maidenhair fern	*Adiantum pedatum*	part shade to shade	loam, acidic, well-drained, moist
Nodding wild onion	*Allium cernuum*	full sun	loam, well-drained, moist
Columbine	*Aquilegia canadensis*	part shade to shade	sand to loam, well-drained, dry to moist
Canada wild ginger	*Asarum canadense*	part shade to shade	loam, moist
Deer fern	*Blechnum spicant*	part shade to shade	loam, moist
Purple poppy mallow	*Callirhoe involucrata*	sun to part shade	all soils, dry to moist
Camas	*Camassia quamash*	full sun	loam to clay, moist
Harebell	*Campanula rotundifolia*	sun, part shade, shade	sandy, well-drained, dry
Coreopsis	*Coreopsis lanceolata*	full sun to shade	sand to clay, well-drained, dry
Purple coneflower	*Echinacea purpurea*	sun to part shade	sand to clay, well-drained, dry
Blanketflower	*Gaillardia aristata*	full sun	sandy to sandy loam, well-drained, dry
Wild geranium	*Geranium maculatum*	part shade to shade	loam, moist
Prairie blazing star	*Liatris pycnostachya*	full sun	sandy loam, well-drained, dry to moist
Columbia lily	*Lilium columbianum*	part shade	loam to sandy loam, dry in summer, moist in spring
Black-eyed Susan	*Rudbeckia hirta*	full sun	sand to loam, well-drained, dry to moist
Prairie dropseed	*Sporobolus heterolepis*	full sun	sandy, dry
Wood poppy	*Stylophorum diphyllum*	part shade to shade	loam, well-drained, moist

NATIVES VS. NATIVARS

Native: A plant that is indigenous to the area. It has developed alongside the native wildlife and is accustomed to the climate, pollinators, and seasonal variations. These plants have been around for hundreds, if not thousands, of years. Many use the term "prior to European settlement" to describe the timeline for a native plant. If it was here before the Europeans were, it's native. They grow, develop, and change through natural means and "natural selection."

The original native → coreopsis is yellow. One hybridized version is yellow and red (below). Many hybridized versions of the coreopsis exist, but are they providing the same nutritional value as the native species?

Nativar: A plant that is based on a native plant (short for "native cultivar"). It has been, however, altered, through human selection. Mutations are very common in plants; the thing with mutations, though, is that they usually don't last naturally. They are a one-off and the following generation is not affected by the changes. Humans often enjoy these mutations (colour changes, flower size or shape, number and placement of petals), so we propagate flowers with characteristics we like.

Research at the University of Vermont has just begun where true natives and nativars (native cultivars) are concerned. Although not published at the time of writing this book, it won't be long. If you are interested in the results, the researchers are Annie White and Leonard Perry.

Let's start with the basics, though. Native plants are open pollinated. They require birds, bees, and other insects, or wind to move pollen between plants. This type of pollination maintains and increases genetic diversity as the pollen grains from one plant move to another and "mingle." Many nativars use what is known as closed pollination, a type of self-pollination, and are propagated vegetatively (not grown from seed); offspring are clones of the parent plant. On top of that, many nativars are sterile, meaning pollination will not result in the production of seeds anyway.

There are benefits to nativars: aesthetically appealing, longer bloom time, drought-tolerance. But do these benefits outweigh the costs? It is currently being researched whether or not the nutritional value of nativars matches their native counterparts and even whether the nativar can attract the pollinators in the first place. Nativars are often selected for their different colours and shapes, which may make it difficult for the pollinators to find and feed from the plant.

Interesting research, indeed. My stance on the matter? If you're restoring a piece of land to its natural habitat, do not use nativars. If you're creating a backyard garden and wildlife habitat, use nativars, but do not use them exclusively. A good mix can be achieved, but it should be a conscious decision to choose native species when trying to build a wildlife-friendly backyard.

2. *Consider mature height*

For plants grown in pots, their maximum potential height at maturity is rarely reached as the size of the pot provides its own limitations to plant growth. For plants grown in gardens, remember that many native wildflowers are perennial, meaning they will keep coming back year after year and will take a few years to grow to their mature height.

Avoid putting very tall plants where they will create too much shade on sun-loving plants; use small, clumping plants for borders; use unique plants as focal points. You will find that many native plants can be considered "focal points," since they are rarely used in the garden. If you like sunflowers, and have the space to grow them, try any of the Silphium family of plants: tall, stable, and perennial. No more replanting year after year. And birds love them.

3. *Use a combination for the greatest effect*

Increasing biodiversity is all about using a variety of plants that bloom throughout the season to provide food, shelter, and breeding habitat for as many species as possible. Pack your small space with as many of these native perennials as you can. Decreasing empty soil space will reduce weeds (fewer weed seeds will make it to the soil to germinate). It will also decrease the need for watering and protect plant roots

← Miscanthus and Echinacea.

on those hot August days. Remember to include native grasses mixed in with your flowers. A grass/flower combo is how nature designs her landscape, and it works well. Or, at least it has for the last several thousand years. Just sayin'.

Here are some combinations that work well together:

For sun:

a. Little bluestem (*Andropogon scoparium*), purple coneflower (*Echinacea purpurea*), butterfly weed (*Asclepias tuberosa*), prairie blazing star (*Liatris pycnostachya*), and showy goldenrod (*Solidago speciosa*)

b. Indiangrass (*Sorghastrum nutans*), pale purple coneflower (*Echinacea pallida*), lanceleaf coreopsis (*Coreopsis lanceolata*), ironweed (*Vernonia fasciculata*), and purple prairie clover (*Dalea purpurea*)

For part shade:

a. Bottlebrush grass (*Elymus hystrix*), wild columbine (*Aquilegia canadensis*), ox-eye sunflower (*Heliopsis helianthoides*), bee balm (*Monarda fistulosa*), golden Alexanders (*Zizia aurea*), New England aster (*Symphyotrichum novae-angliae*), and black-eyed Susan (*Rudbeckia hirta*)

b. Virginia rye (*Elymus virginicus*), spiderwort (*Tradescantia ohiensis*), sweet Joe-pye weed (*eupatorium purpureum*), culver's root (*Veronicastrum virginicum*), yellow coneflower (*Ratibida pinnata*), and branched coneflower (*Rudbeckia triloba*)

Start by growing "patches" and they will find their own favourite spots in your garden. The meadow experience (gardening with grasses and flowers) is all about learning to accept losses, knowing that Nature is working on her own terms. The gains in the end will greatly outweigh the losses you may experience.

4. Colour

Some gardeners are very particular about colour and others couldn't care less. As long as you remember to include something to bloom in each season (to feed pollinators from spring to fall), you can be as colour picky as you wish.

5. *Bring in some non-natives*

I like to experiment with natives and non-natives, perennials and annuals. I mix them up each year by planting some different non-native annuals that will brighten up dull spots in the garden while the perennial natives are gearing up to put on their show. There's no reason why your garden can't be a combination of the two.

6. *Plan for pollinators*

The following table will give you some ideas of great pollinator-friendly plants that are native to Canada. I have also included their native province, if planting "locally native" is important to you. Personally, I believe that if a plant is native to North America, and it can survive in your yard, it is worth considering. Many native plant enthusiasts believe that only plants native to the local area are safe to plant and healthy for the pollinators. Whichever side of the fence you're on, do your best to make your garden, patio, or balcony attractive to pollinators and beneficial insects.

THIS PAGE: Joe-pye weed. OPPOSITE: My "wild" flower garden. →

POLLINATOR-FRIENDLY PLANTS

Common Name	Latin Name	Native Province	What You Can Expect to Attract
Anise hyssop	*Agastache foeniculum*	BC, AB, SK, MB, ON, QC, NWT, NB, NS	bees, butterflies, soldier beetles
Leadplant	*Amorpha canescens*	MB, ON	bees, butterflies
Pasque flower	*Anemone patens*	BC, AB, SK, MB, ON, YK, NWT	early spring bees, bee flies, syrphid flies
Butterfly weed	*Asclepias tuberosa*	ON, QC	butterflies, bees, wasps, beetles
Purple prairie clover	*Dalea purpurea*	AB, SK, MB, ON	bees, syrphid flies, beetles
Purple coneflower	*Echinacea purpurea*	ON	butterflies, bees, beetles, hummingbirds
(spotted) Joe-pye weed	*Eupatorium maculatum/ Eutrochium maculatum*	BC, AB, SK, MB, ON, QC, NB, NS, PEI, NFLD	butterflies, bees, moths
Downy sunflower	*Helianthus mollis*	ON	bees, bee flies, butterflies
Prairie blazing star	*Liatris pycnostachya*	QC, NB	bees, moths (tiger moth uses as host plant), butterflies, bee flies, syrphid flies
Wild lupine	*Lupinus perennis*	ON, NFLD	bees, syrphid flies, larval host plant for many butterfly species
Bee balm	*Monarda fistulosa*	BC, AB, SK, MB, ON, QC, NWT	wasps, bees, bee flies, beetles, butterflies, hummingbird moth, larval host plant for several moth species
Wild quinine	*Parthenium integrifolium*	No native Canadian range but will survive well into zone 5	bees, especially sweat bees, wasps, butterflies, moths, ants, spiders, syrphid flies
Branched coneflower	*Rudbeckia triloba*	ON, QC	self-pollinating but nectar attracts bees, butterflies, syrphid flies, bee flies
Prairie dock	*Silphium terebinthinaceum*	ON	bees, butterflies
Stiff goldenrod	*Solidago rigida*	AB, SK, MB, ON	bees, flies, wasps, butterflies, syrphid flies, tachinid flies, beetles. Excellent fall food.
Showy goldenrod	*Solidago speciosa*	ON	bees, butterflies, wasps, syrphid flies. Excellent late-season food.
Hoary vervain	*Verbena stricta*	ON, QC	bees, butterflies, syrphid flies, bee flies, beetles
Ironweed	*Vernonia fasciculata*	MB	bees, syrphid flies, butterflies, beetles
Golden Alexanders	*Zizia aurea*	MB, ON, QC, NB, NS	bees, syrphid flies, butterflies, beetles, ladybeetles

WATER IN THE GARDEN

Water features in your yard are your best opportunity to increase biodiversity. Not only do they provide drinking and feeding opportunities for a number of birds, mammals, and amphibians, they also provide an entirely unique ecosystem for attracting wildlife that need water for all or part of their life.

Even a small pond can add significantly to the "wild" activity that occurs in your yard. What if I told you that by devoting two square metres of your space to water, you could create breeding habitat for dragonflies, salamanders, newts, and small frogs, provided it has some established greenery growing in and around it? It's true — you don't need a huge space for a pond, you just need to be smart and creative about it.

My yard has a pond with koi in it. The fish overwinter, breed, and splash around daily when I go out to feed them. My pond has been around for a number of years and the wild creatures remember, returning to my yard each spring. We have countless tadpoles come spring, and frogs in summer (and they do actually sit on lily pads!), many salamander and newt nymphs that are 100 percent waterlogged until they grow legs and stroll onto the land (they're similar to frogs in that way), and a plethora of insect species that use the pond as a breeding ground. My fish, meantime, nibble happily at the squirmy mosquito larvae. Turns out, fish are the answer to the number one objection to ponds: they have a huge appetite for the larvae.

A pond ecosystem is a tad more complex than the garden ecosystem. There are a number of factors to consider, including water quality, escape routes for wildlife, proper vegetation, and the overall water system. Here is a list that you should consider before installing a garden pond.

1. *Water quality*

This is extremely important. Avoid filling your pond with tap water as municipal water has been treated with some sort of chemical (chlorine, no doubt). Instead, use a rain barrel to collect water or purchase chemical neutralizers from the local garden retailer or pond [not "pawn"] shop. Regular chlorine used to treat city water can evaporate off on a hot day, leaving the water safe for plant and animal species, but some municipalities use chemicals (chloramines, in particular) that do not work this way. This is when those neutralizers can be effective in preparing your garden pond for wildlife.

2. *Escape routes*

Pond edges can be a welcome invitation for numerous species of wildlife. If raccoons are a concern [BEWARE, they love to eat fish!] then design your pond with steep, sloping sides so that a raccoon cannot dip his paws into the water and scoop up a meal. If you are putting in steep slopes, make sure there is a flat edge at the bottom of the slope or several large rocks

↑ Dragonflies are one of the first insects you'll attract with the introduction of a water feature.

that are only partially submerged so amphibians can rest. Keep water clean to avoid sludge building up on hard surfaces. Use floating plants for extra resting places and oxygenating plants, which will help to keep the water clear.

3. *Proper vegetation*

Use plants that are not invasive, aren't going to completely cover the pond's surface, and ones that will provide wildlife with food, shelter, and long-term habitat. I've provided a list of native pond plants that will fit the profile. It's important to provide plants that float, that root to the pond's bottom layers, and that grow around the pond's perimeter. Perimeter plants, or "marginals," provide nesting habitat for some birds,

shelter and shade for turtles, frogs, and toads, and the roots help to secure the pond's edges.

Ideally, your pond surface will be covered 60 percent by shade, foliage, and flowers, while 40 percent remains open to sunshine. This is an important step toward creating the perfect balance in your pond for desirable wildlife and plants.

4. *The complete system*

There are a number of ways you can build a pond and, in the end, it will depend on you. Cost, space, and the time it takes you to install and maintain your pond are all important factors. There are several types of ponds, each of which will meet these requirements in a different way.

↑ My "Canadian" garden pond.

POND PLANT LIST

Common Name	Latin Name	Habitat Preference*
Blue flag iris	*Iris versicolor*	pond edge
Blue vervain	*Verbena hastata*	pond edge
Cardinal flower	*Lobelia cardinalis*	pond edge
Elderberry	*Sambucus canadensis*	pond edge
Joe-pye weed	*Eutrochium maculatum*	pond edge
Marsh marigold	*Caltha palustris*	pond edge
Swamp milkweed	*Asclepias incarnata*	pond edge
Turtlehead	*Chelone glabra*	pond edge
Broadleaf arrowhead	*Sagittaria latifolia*	shallow
Common mare's tail	*Hippuris vulgaris*	shallow
Marsh cinquefoil	*Comarum palustre*	shallow
Pickerelweed	*Pontederia cordata*	shallow
Water plantain	*Alisma triviale*	shallow
Wild rice	*Zizania palustris*	shallow
American water plantain	*Alisma triviale Alisma plantago-aquatica*	surface
Floating pondweed	*Polygonum amphibium*	surface
Water knotweed	*Polygonum amphibium*	surface
Water smartweed	*Polygonum amphibium*	surface
Watermeal	*Wolffia columbiana Wolffia borealis*	surface
Watershield	*Brasenia schreberi*	surface
White water lily	*Nymphaea odorata*	surface
Yellow water lily	*Nuphar variegatum*	surface
Canadian waterweed	*Elodea canadensis*	submerged
Common bladderwort	*Utricularia vulgaris*	submerged
Coontail	*Ceratophyllum demersum*	submerged
Nuttall's waterweed	*Elodea nuttallii*	submerged
Water moss	*Fontinalis antipyretica*	submerged
Water milfoil	*Myriophyllum exalbescens*	submerged
Water nymph	*Najas flexilis*	submerged
White water buttercup	*Ranunculus aquatilis*	submerged

*Pond edge: roots are not directly in the water but prefers moist conditions; **Marginal**: at the pond's edge, prefers shallow water; **Surface**: either floats on the surface or is rooted but only partially submerged; **Submerged**: completely underwater, either rooted or loose.

Natural Ponds

These are essentially holes in the ground (lined, usually). They contain no filtration system and no movement of water. They require a significant amount of greenery (in and around the pond) to keep stagnation at bay. Note: more fish contained in your pond [and the larger the fish] translates to more organic matter that needs to be flushed clean or neutralized by oxygenators. Excess fish poop can encourage algae growth. One way around this is to introduce barley straw into your pond. The straw, as it breaks down, releases some sort of chemical (no one is entirely sure how this works yet) that puts a stop to algae growth. Be careful, though, as too much of the stuff can kill fish. Consult with a local expert about the right amount for your pond as it will depend on a few factors.

Waterfall Ponds

These are similar to the natural pond, but the water moves. Often, a waterfall pond contains multiple levels (creating the waterfall effect) and doesn't require as many plants to keep the water fresh. Water is oxygenated as it moves through the different levels and over undulating rocks. You will need a pump and a filter. If you choose to go this route, make sure you talk to a professional to determine which pump is best for your pond, as there are many factors that come into play when trying to move water. If you don't want multiple levels but are interested in moving the water, skip the waterfall and just use a pump to create a water fountain effect. With ever-increasing interest in backyard ponds, finding the right system has never been easier. An experienced water-feature specialist can be worth their weight in gold in terms of the advice that they give. Look for a good one at your local garden retailer or ask if they can recommend one in your community.

Ephemeral Ponds

Some people choose to let nature take care of everything when it comes to their pond. These are called ephemeral ponds (or vernal pools) because they are wet after it rains and dry when a drought hits. Ephemeral ponds are a common occurrence in nature where the soil can hold water for a period of time but the depression is not quite deep enough to ward off complete evaporation. Many insects and amphibious creatures benefit from ponds like these where no fish can survive and so no predation can occur. In many areas, a natural ephemeral pond is likely difficult to achieve due to improper soil conditions (an ephemeral pond needs a clay base to hold the water) but in areas where it will work, you may be surprised by just how much life actually exists within.

Many land developers and city planners are looking at ephemeral ponds on a broader scale to help manage stormwater. "Bioswales" can save municipalities a lot of money in terms of stormwater management simply by filtering the water through a man-made natural catchment system.

Water Features for Very Small Spaces

If you have no room for a pond, there are other water features that can be just as accommodating. Think bird baths with moving features that deter mosquito larvae but allow birds to bathe and drink easily. If you have a railing, consider a hanging water bath or one that sits atop the railing. They don't take up extra room and are readily available from a number of commercial retailers. Find one that suits your style and keep it filled with clean water. Clean water is extremely important (change it every day) to avoid birds spreading diseases to one another. The same goes for feeders, while we're on the subject — you should be cleaning them out once a week (including hummingbird feeders).

For Those Very High Up

If you have to look up, *waaaaay* up, to see your balcony, it's likely that birds that use baths aren't doing too much flying that high. You do have options, though. If your building has a communal green space, consider speaking with the superintendant or building manager about starting a bird-friendly habitat. Not only does it attract the birds and provide them with a safe place to drink and bathe, it will give you, and others, a place to relax and watch them. And if that option doesn't pan out, be sure to take some time to visit a local water feature to enjoy the sights and sounds.

↑ If you can't have your own water feature, visit a public one.

↑ A backyard pond with moving water is an excellent option, and finding the right system has never been easier.

CREATING BIRD AND BUTTERFLY HABITAT

Your backyard, balcony, or patio space can be bird and butterfly friendly with the use of some fairly simple features:

1. *Berry trees/bushes*

If you have a bit more space, consider planting a tree or shrub that will flower and produce berries or other small fruit. The flowers will attract butterflies and other pollinators. Crabapple, raspberry, blueberry, serviceberry, elderberry, dogwood, and spicebush are excellent providers of edible fruit to feed the birds. Of course, this list is nowhere near complete, and I would encourage you to visit your local garden centre to find a berry-producing plant that will work for your particular growing zone.

Some small understory plants will also produce berries and would be good for areas that do not receive a lot of sun. Smooth Solomon's seal, false Solomon's seal, Jack-in-the-pulpit, mayapple, columbine, Joe-pye weed, and turtle-head, to name a few.

If vertical space is all you have, consider a Kiwi (*Actinidia kolomikta*) for full sun, porcelain vine (*Ampelopsis brevipedunculata* 'Elegans') for part shade, and climbing hydrangea (*Hydrangea anomala* subsp. *petiolaris*) for shade. Not all of these will produce edible berries, but they will provide nectar for butterflies and a sheltered spot to rest for just about any small critter.

↑ Elderberry.

↑ TOP: Jack-in-the-Pulpit. BOTTOM: My kiwi vine.

2. *Nectar plants*

Butterflies and hummingbirds will thank you for plants that provide an ongoing source of nectar. Pollen and nectar will also attract a range of pollinators looking for food and nest-building materials. Provide three seasons of nectar for best results.

↑ Lantana.

↑ Campanula rotundifolia (harebell)..

NECTAR PLANTS

Common Name	Latin Name	Bloom Time	Native?
FLOWERING PLANTS			
Bee balm	*Monarda fistulosa*	Summer–Fall	Yes
Butterfly weed	*Asclepias tuberosa*	Summer	Yes
Cardinal flower	*Lobelia cardinalis*	Summer	Yes
Cup plant	*Silphium perfoliatum*	Summer–Fall	Yes
Harebell	*Campanula rotundifolia*	Summer	Yes
Hollyhock	*Alcea rosea*	Summer–Fall	No
Hosta	*Hosta* spp.	Summer	No
Lantana	*Lantana camara*	Summer–Fall	No
New England aster	*Symphyotrichum novae-angliae*	Fall	Yes
New York aster	*Symphyotrichum novi-belgii*	Fall	Yes
Obedient plant	*Physostegia virginiana*	Summer–Fall	Yes
Purple prairie clover	*Dalea purpurea*	Summer	Yes
Rhodora	*Rhododendron canadense*	Spring–Summer	Yes
Sky-blue aster	*Symphyotrichum oolentangiense*	Fall	Yes
Smooth aster	*Symphyotrichum laeve*	Fall	Yes
Turtlehead	*Chelone lyonii; Chelone glabra*	Summer–Fall	Yes
Virginia bluebells	*Mertensia virginica*	Spring	Yes
White aster	*Oligoneuron album*	Fall	Yes
Wild columbine	*Aquilegia canadensis*	Spring–Summer	Yes
TREES AND SHRUBS			
Black twinberry	*Lonicera involucrata*	Spring–Summer	Yes
Flowering dogwood	*Cornus florida*	Spring	Yes
Hairy manzanita	*Arctostaphylos columbiana*	Early Spring	Yes (BC)
Red flowering currant	*Ribes sanguineum*	Early Spring	Yes (BC)
Thimbleberry	*Rubus parviflorus*	Spring	Yes

3. Seed plants

This one is for the birds — butterflies could care less if your plants provide seeds. It will depend on the birds in your area, but generally birds are interested in seeds that are a decent size. Seeds that could be mistaken for a powdery dust aren't really worth their time. Here are some North American natives that are sure to please the birds. Keep them standing throughout the winter to provide cover and a source of food. Not to mention, it gives you something to look at.

- coneflower (*Echinacea* spp.)
- black-eyed Susan (*Rudbeckia hirta*)
- sunflower (*Helianthus* spp.)
- compassplant (*Silphium laciniatum*)
- cup plant (*Silphium perfoliatum*)
- prairie dock (*Silphium terebinthinaceum*)
- yellow coneflower (*Ratibida pinnata*)
- bee balm (*Monarda fistulosa*)
- Indiangrass (*Sorghastrum nutans*)
- little bluestem (*Schizachyrium scoparium*)
- big bluestem (*Andropogon gerardii*)
- New England aster (*Symphyotrichum novae-angliae*)
- sky blue aster (*Symphyotrichum oolentangiense*)

↑ Sunflower.

↑ Black-eyed Susans.

4. Shade/coverage/protection

Providing coverage can be as simple as installing a birdhouse or nesting box, or it can be more extravagant with the planting of evergreen trees and bushes that double as landscape features while providing year-round coverage. Many birds overwinter in Canada, despite the cold weather, and no doubt appreciate the respite provided by some natural features.

If you choose to put up houses or nest boxes for the birds, face the open side away from the prevailing winds. Same goes for butterfly houses, which can be bought or made. The houses should have a roof to keep water from dripping in, and they should be made from natural materials (wood instead of plastic, for example).

If you are trying to attract certain birds, you will need to look into the type of house that particular bird prefers and their favourite food sources. I have provided you with a good start, but with more than 400 birds in Canada, it's only a start. This chart will tell you what kind of food they prefer and where they like to hang out in the winter. The column titled "Where You'll See Them" denotes their preferred habitat, which, in some cases, includes your backyard. Once you have established the birds that are visiting your yard, then you can start to provide housing.

↑ You can put up nesting boxes, but you may end up with birds nesting in other places. Do your best to accommodate them and relocate the nest after the babies have flown off.

5. Watering holes/mud holes

Bird baths that are kept free from mildew and aren't becoming a regular mosquito breeding ground are excellent for birds, but butterflies require a different type of liquid: mud. A puddle with a sandy bottom located in a sunny area is perfect for butterflies, which use their long tongue-like mouth piece called a proboscis to drink up the liquid. It's actually called "puddling" (aptly named). They will also tap into liquid that collects in or on plants. Cup plants provide an excellent water source in an interesting way.

↑ Cup plant holding water.

6. Feeders

Shopping for a bird feeder or scouring the Internet for building instructions can be daunting. With so many options available, it's hard to know which is best for you. My advice? Get something easy to clean and within your budget. There's no need to break the bank for the best feeder on the market. With that said, you do want to go with glass over plastic whenever you can (easier to clean and it lasts longer). Wood feeders are great, too, but ensure that if they are the "house"-type feeder, there is a good amount of drainage to keep the water from pooling inside, which can enable disease to spread and eventually mould to grow.

When you buy (or build) a feeder, know what will be feeding from it and buy the seed to match. There's no use buying a peanut feeder if you want to feed the finches (who need smaller seeds like black oil sunflower or nyjer). I would suggest using a few different types of feeders. A tube feeder is great because it takes up very little space, but many birds cannot hang from it to eat and many are too large. With that said, I really enjoy my upside-down suet feeder, which attracts, among others, hairy and downy woodpeckers. A great all-purpose feeder with suet cages attached will provide a source of food for the largest variety of birds.

Hummingbird feeders are growing in popularity. Again, keeping them clean is of upmost importance. Mould grows quickly in a hummingbird feeder and the small spaces make them more difficult to clean. Empty and rinse out your hummingbird feeder once a week. Refill it and hang it near flowers they will enjoy. Hummingbirds particularly like plants with tube-shaped flowers (cardinal flower, hosta, and obedient plant are a few examples). *(Note: at least one species of hummingbird is native to all provinces, except Newfoundland, though my sources tell me that there are rare sightings when they are blown off the mainland in a storm. Otherwise, Newfoundlanders must content themselves with an abundance of moose — far more per capita than any other province.)*

For the butterflies, plants are all you need. I wouldn't go out of my way to get a feeder for a butterfly, but be sure you're planting a range of flowers as some are finicky, feeding from one particular plant, while others are generalists. Flat-topped flowers, like *Echinacea* spp. and *Coreopsis* spp., are used as a food source and a resting place.

Types of seed. Clockwise from top left: cracked corn, nyjer, raw oats, black oil sunflower, hulled sunflower, hulled peanuts, safflower, and millet. →

Upside-down suet feeder. Great! Blackbirds hate them, because they can't eat upside down. ↑

Be sure to keep your bird feeders as far away from your bird/butterfly garden as possible. Some birds will eat butterflies, but if you keep them preoccupied with their own source of food for the summer, they are more likely to stay out of the garden area. In the fall, birds will visit the garden area looking for seeds and berries but the moths and butterflies will have begun to overwinter.

The scientists who study such things as biodiversity and its prevalence in urban environments have stated that as human density increases, urban biodiversity decreases. It makes sense, really: more of us means less room for anything else. There's no reason we can't make our spaces at least a little accommodating, though.

One of the hardest things to do when trying to enrich your space for wildlife is sourcing the materials. The discussion between hybrid and non-hybridized plants is ongoing, and generally those who have an opinion are not fence-sitters. I believe there is room for both. Same goes for non-natives (provided they stay where they're put). A combination can provide your space with lasting colour, seasonal interest, and, of course, plenty of food for any wandering birds and bees looking for a meal.

Seasonal interest is so important for wildlife. Overwintering birds seek out food from perennial seed heads, berries from trees, and native grasses. Overwintering insects require places to spend the winter safely protected from winds and cold temperatures. Our autumn gardening habits can either help or hinder these life cycles. Let's help them by learning how to prepare the garden for the winter.

↑ Hummingbirds love hosta flowers. I hang a hummingbird feeder above my largest hosta plant and see them buzzing around all day.

Species	Preferred Food		Where You'll See Them	Winter Location
American goldfinch	black oil sunflower hulled sunflower	nyjer	woodlots, open fields, orchards, backyards	southern parts of eastern Canada; the southernmost portion of British Columbia/Alberta border
American robin	fruit hulled sunflower peanuts (shelled)	mealworms suet	fields, woodlots, forests, backyards	overwinters across southern Canada and coastal British Columbia
Black-capped chickadee	black oil sunflower hulled sunflower mealworms nyjer	peanuts safflower suet	trees and woody shrubs, marshes with tall, sturdy vegetation	overwinters across Canada
Blue jay	black oil sunflower cracked corn fruit hulled sunflower suet	mealworms peanuts safflower millet	forest edges, forests with an abundance of oak trees	overwinters from eastern Canada to Alberta
Bohemian waxwing	fruit (oranges are popular)		boreal forests, forest edges, semi-open areas, orchards, and yards where fruit trees are abundant	overwinters across Canada
Cedar waxwing	fruit		woodlands and orchards, backyards with fruiting trees	overwinters across southern Canada
Chestnut-backed chickadee	black oil sunflower hulled sunflower mealworms nyjer	peanuts safflower suet	coniferous forests, city parks, backyard trees	coastal British Columbia and somewhat into southern Alberta
Common redpoll	black oil sunflower hulled sunflower	nyjer	open and weedy fields, conifer forests	overwinters across Canada
Dark-eyed junco	black oil sunflower cracked corn hulled sunflower millet	nyjer oats (uncooked) peanuts (shelled) safflower	coniferous and mixed forests, open woodlands, backyards, and fields	overwinters across southern Canada
Downy woodpecker	black oil sunflower hulled sunflower mealworms	peanuts safflower suet	open woodlands, weedy forest edges, parks, backyards, orchards	overwinters across Canada

OVERWINTERING BIRDS				
Species	**Preferred Food**		**Where You'll See Them**	**Winter Location**
Evening grosbeak	black oil sunflower	hulled sunflower	backyards, forests	overwinters across Canada
Hairy woodpecker	black oil sunflower hulled sunflower mealworms	peanuts safflower suet	mature forests, woodlots, parks, forest edges, and bug-infested forests	overwinters across Canada
Hoary redpoll	black oil sunflower hulled sunflower	nyjer	woodland edges, open or weedy fields	overwinters across Canada
Mountain chickadee	black oil sunflower hulled sunflower mealworms nyjer	peanuts safflower suet	dry forests, mountainous areas, prefers evergreen trees	western Canada
Mourning dove	black oil sunflower cracked corn hulled sunflower millet	nyjer oats (uncooked) peanuts (shelled) safflower	open fields, single trees	southern parts of eastern Canada, southern parts of British Columbia
Northern cardinal	black oil sunflower cracked corn hulled sunflower	millet peanuts (shelled) safflower	forest edges, backyards, woodlots; prefer semi-open areas with plenty of shrubby brush	eastern Canada
Pine warbler	hulled sunflower mealworms	peanuts (shelled) suet	coniferous trees	eastern Canada
Red-breasted nuthatch	black oil sunflower hulled sunflower mealworms	peanuts suet	coniferous forests	overwinters across Canada
Red-winged blackbird	black oil sunflower cracked corn hulled sunflower	millet oats (uncooked) peanuts (shelled)	near wetlands and other water sources; can also be found in open meadow areas	coastal British Columbia, southern Ontario, southern Nova Scotia
White-breasted nuthatch	black oil sunflower hulled sunflower mealworms	peanuts safflower suet	woodland edges	overwinters across Canada

![maple leaf] CLEANING UP (OR NOT) TO INCREASE BIODIVERSITY

Yesterday's gardener is what some people would term a "clean freak." Maniacal, almost obsessive garden cleanup come autumn, however, is no way to encourage and support wildlife. Tall stems are filled with seeds, the dropped fruit are carbohydrate-packed gold mines for birds, and the foliage that will rot away over the winter into spring is home to hundreds of insects and larvae that will grow and become food for others (not to mention, return good old-fashioned nutrients to the soil as they break down).

The winter garden can be an ugly place. An ugly, snow-covered expanse with no visible signs of life, save for a few of the braver birds and panicky squirrels. That is, if you cut everything down in the fall. Winter interest is a term used a lot in gardening circles in Canada. Gardeners appreciate just about anything that reminds us of the greener seasons, so that tall but robust coneflower stem is a welcome contrast to the blindingly bright white of a fresh snowfall. In its own way, the seed head of a perennial or a sunflower poking through the snow is attractive.

Some plants are best composted in the fall and others are best left in the garden. There's no one-shot recipe for this. I could not say to you: cut all annuals to the ground and leave all perennials. Here are my recommendations where fall garden prep is concerned:

Hosta: I tend to leave 15-20 centimetres of the hosta stem. You can certainly leave them with no repercussions, I just find they turn to complete mush by the spring. I use a sharp pair of pruners or long-bladed shears (depending on the size of the hosta) and just snip away the foliage. It will turn to a pulp in the composter after a few frosts.

Coneflowers: I leave these standing. They have strong stems that can withstand wind and some snow. Eventually they will be covered in most areas with heavy snow, but in the early days of winter, they will feed the birds and give you something to look at.

Ornamental Grasses: I have a couple hundred ornamental grasses in my garden that look great all winter. They blow in the breeze, their seed heads accumulate snow, and birds forage for the seeds all winter long. What's not to like? Dried grasses make an almost eerie sound when they're blowing in the winter wind, and, of course, they are a favourite for the birds. Not only do they

Seed heads covered in snow provide visual interest in the winter garden. →

THE NEW CANADIAN GARDEN

↑ Grasses add winter interest to the garden.

provide food, they offer refuge from chilly winds. I cut them down almost to the ground in April, leaving about 10 centimetres standing.

Annuals (non-bulb): The non-bulb annuals I buy or grow from seed are usually small (pansies, petunias, begonias, zinnias by the hundreds, New Guinea impatiens). They provide a shot of colour while perennials are growing into theirs during the summer. Some of them I leave and they will break down over winter and some are replaced with more seasonal fall counterparts. I clear the finished flowering plants each fall from my window boxes, balcony hangers, and patio planters.

Annuals (bulb/tubers): Some bulbs, like dahlias and caladiums, are perennial in their native region, but annual here. If left over winter, they will freeze and die. I dig them up, rub off the soil, and let them dry out. I leave them in a cool, dark place over the winter and replant them in the spring.

Spring-Flowering Bulb Perennials: Lilies, tulips, and daffodils sprout from a bulb beginning in early spring. For tulips, daffodils, and other early-spring flowers, I wait six weeks after they have finished blooming then take a clean, sharp hoe and cut them down eight to ten centimetres from the ground (you can also use pruners or shears). I compost the foliage knowing that the plant has used the six weeks post-flowering to manufacture its own food through the miracle of photosynthesis. No need to dig up these bulbs (if only someone would tell that to the squirrels).

By the way, if you wish to plant spring-flowering bulbs and avoid the squirrel problem, plant narcissus and daffodils. They hate them!

Roses: I always buy roses that have been grown close to home as they are more tolerant of the seasonal conditions where I live. I would advise you to do the same. I mound up about 50 centimetres of garden soil or triple mix at the base of the rose to protect the roots and the rose crown over the winter. If the stems of the rose stand more than a metre high, they may get blown around in the wind: I cut the long stems down to about a metre in the fall; otherwise I leave all pruning until the spring.

Clematis: For this, it's best to know what kind of clematis you have. There are three basic categories: spring-blooming, repeat bloomers, summer/fall blooming. I prune spring bloomers back in the spring after they have finished flowering to ensure they have enough time to develop new wood and

↑ Pansies.

↑ Canadian rose ('Bonica rose') — one of my favourites.

buds for next spring. Often they repeat a set of blossoms later in the same year.

I prune repeat bloomers in the spring but I do so carefully — only taking away dead growth — and I comb my fingers through the twisted stems to remove the dead, dry material from last year. Fall-blooming clematis is pruned early in the spring. Some years I take the "do nothing" approach, especially if I want the clematis to grow up a trellis or provide a sort of privacy fence, which can take a few years. There's no harm in not doing anything, but some clematis varieties will grow extremely fast and seem to swallow the trellis.

Vegetables: The soft-crop vegetables should be pulled out and put into the composter to break down over the winter. It is amazing how much composting goes on through a Canadian winter, especially in areas with distinct freeze/thaw cycles.

Leafy vegetables like lettuce, kale, and pak choi will break down quickly. Tomatoes, peppers, corn, and carrots take longer due to their thick stems and deep roots. You can take everything that is left over in the veggie garden come fall and lay it on top of the soil for the winter. The material will break down, nutrients will move back into the soil, and what remains big and bulky in the spring can be picked up and composted or turned under.

↑ Curly leaf lettuce can look ornamental.

↑ My clematis.

117

🍁 THE IMPORTANCE OF HEALTHY SOIL

Modern farming practices have led us to believe that there is a "no-till" solution to gardening. It is true that turning your soil over with a spade or a Rototiller causes dramatic changes in the soil and disturbs beneficial microbes, mycorrhizae, and insects. For the most part, I avoid turning my soil over. However, where weeds need to be brought under control mid to late spring, a light turning over with a Rototiller can save a lot of work (weeding) later in the season.

In my garden, I till my vegetable garden annually, just lightly, working in some fresh duck manure or mushroom compost each season. The soil on my property is clay loam and is difficult to work after the weight of the snow and ice has compacted it. My solution is to add generous quantities of sharp builder's sand and compost — I find a 70 percent compost to 30 percent sand mix is ideal.

The addition of finished manure and compost each year is a long-term commitment to healthy soil. In areas where I won't be putting down manure or compost (where the carrots will go, for example), I use a sharp hoe to mix in sand where clay makes planting difficult.

If your soil is not clay-based, you do not *need* to till. Tilling does disturb the soil structure, breaks the surface crust that holds soil in place, and disturbs worm and other insect habitat. With that said, though, if you have a heavy infestation of soil-borne insects, like potato beetles or cut worms, a light tilling of the veggie garden may reduce your numbers in the spring. I do not recommend that you use heavy equipment soon after a rain, as this increases soil compaction and will reduce your soil's porosity, leaving less open space for oxygen and water. The same goes for any activity early in spring. Allow your soil to dry about five centimetres deep before you work it or even walk on it. Your patience will pay off!

Here's a short how-to for the no-till and till methods I employ on my property.

The No-Till Approach

The no-till areas in my garden are mainly located in the parts of the garden that contain annual and perennial flowers. I keep digging to a minimum when putting in new plants and add a generous shovel or two of compost into the hole at the time of planting.

When starting a new garden bed, there are many no-till options. Unless you have moved into a new house and sod/grass seed has yet to be put down, you're likely dealing with a thick mat of thin green blades where you'd like to see a garden. Tilling is an option, of course, but it is energy intensive and fairly destructive. If you have chosen an area where you wish to create a new garden bed, here are three alternatives to tilling that will take some effort on your part at the beginning but will be much healthier for the soil:

1. **Lay down boards, cardboard, old rugs,** or anything that will block out the sunlight. Create the shape you'd like the garden to be and leave the material in place for six weeks. By then the grass should be dead and you can

Weed-free straw can be used to block out sunlight when creating a new garden bed. The straw can be left in place afterward. ↑

prepare the soil for planting. Keeping plants close together will shade out weeds.

2. **Lay down 15-20 centimetres (6-8 inches) of weed-free straw** over the area you wish to make a garden. The straw effectively does the same thing as the boards I mentioned above (blocks out sunlight). The difference is that the straw stays in place and is used as mulch: you plant right into it. Once the grass underneath is brown, part the straw where you want to put plants, dig a hole just big enough for the plant, and pull the straw back around the plant once it is in the ground. Seeds will not work well with this method (at least not at first), and you'll find that buying seedlings or starting your own seeds is most effective. Over time, the straw will break down and seeds may be used. Note: be sure that you use "clean" seed-free straw.

3. **Use fallen leaves as mulch.** Spread dry, loose fallen leaves about 50 centimetres thick (or 20 centimetres if they are wet and matted down). Sticks and twigs are okay, too, and do not worry about leaf decomposition. Oak leaves break down slowly, but that just means you will be returning nutrients back to the soil for a greater period of time. Once the leaves have smothered

the grass, plant using the same method mentioned above for straw: just part the leaves and plant. In the spring, you may need to pull some small tree seedlings that have started to grow.

Digging, Double-Digging, and Rototilling

These methods are labour-intensive. Remember that you are disturbing the soil, creating the potential for erosion if the area is sloped and it becomes windy or rainy after the soil has been worked. Try to time your soil manipulation around any adverse weather conditions that could increase erosion. If you can't work it all at once without meeting with heavy rains or windstorms, work in sections. Work a small area, plant it, and then begin work on another area. Don't let the soil sit bare for longer than a few days.

GARDEN TOOLS

Sharper tools = easier work. Want to minimize the effort that it takes to dig a hole or cut down weeds? Make sure that you use sharp tools. Here in Canada we buy dull tools from almost all garden retailers (including Home Hardware, where my own line is offered!). The reason that a shovel, spade, or hoe is not pre-sharpened is that accidents can happen before the sale of a tool; in Japan, however, the opposite is true. Most digging and weeding tools are pre-sharpened and sold with a plastic wrap for protection.

When you buy a tool that needs sharpening, either put an edge on it by using a grinding wheel or pay the knife and scissor sharpener who drives round the neighbourhood each spring to do it for you. Then maintain the edge by using a garden file each time you take the tool outside for use. You will be impressed at how much easier the work becomes!

↑ Leaves make excellent natural mulch and return nutrients to the soil at the same time.

LEFT: Tools of the trade. →
RIGHT: Double digging. →

If you are digging a new garden by hand, I suggest that you use a sturdy spade and a comfortable pair gardening gloves. Blisters will happen without them. I would also invest in a file to keep your shovel sharp (and really, all your tools that require a sharp blade).

Digging

Exactly as it sounds. Use a shovel to dig up the material you don't want anymore. Use the shovel to turn over bare soil and remove perennial weeds (along with their root systems). Use a hard rake to smooth out the soil after you have turned it over and screened out the weeds. Work in some finished compost: about 40 kilos per square metre is not too much!

You can use a sod cutter to remove expanses of grass, but again, these are labour-intensive machines and may be expensive to rent. However you decide to remove the grass, I suggest that you put the grass into the composter by placing it there upside down. It will rot in a couple of months. There is no sense throwing out all the free nitrogen in the grass blades and the organic matter in the root zone of the sod. If you don't have a composter, consider setting up a small one in the corner of the yard, even if it's just a place to put the mats of grass.

Double Digging

Double digging requires the removal of the grass or top layer, then the secondary layer. The third layer is "turned over," and as you backfill with the second layer again, you mix it with compost. You will need enough compost to build the new garden up above grade by a maximum of 30 centimetres.

Soil that has been worked to this degree is susceptible to serious compaction. To avoid this, work the area in sections small enough for you to keep from walking or kneeling in the disturbed soil. Plant in worked sections by standing and kneeling on undisturbed sections or by placing wooden boards down on the garden bed to displace your weight evenly.

Rototilling

You will likely need to rent the equipment for this task. The depth to which you till is entirely up to you. I generally till no deeper than five centimetres (two inches) and I find that many weeds are brought to the surface. Before I till, I try to remove weeds that can reproduce through the tiniest root fragments (on my property, Canada thistle and twitch grass are enemy number one and two). Tilling these weeds only helps to propagate more of them. After removing them, roots and all, I then go back over the area to pull large clumps of grass or other weeds, trying to get as much of the root system as possible. Of course, all of this material can go into the composter. Perennials weeds will persist even if composted, unless they have been "cooked" at temperatures of up to 140°C (which isn't actually difficult to achieve in a proper composting system).

Raised Beds and Pots

The soil in your raised beds should be weed-free and near "perfect." Fill them with "new" soil purchased from the garden retailer and make sure that the soil mix is of good quality. Sometimes the best way to tell is to buy from a source and a brand that you trust! It will be a combination of quality ingredients: perlite, peat moss, calcined clay (used to retain moisture), slow-release fertilizer, and, ideally, worm castings.

In an established raised bed, tilling isn't necessary and, indeed, you will likely find it difficult. If you'd like to work the top layer of soil, use a sharp, clean hoe and just drag it lightly over the surface. Each spring, replace the top 15 centimetres of soil in containers and raised beds with fresh container mix. I prefer Pro-Mix or my own Mark's Choice container mix, but there are other quality mixes available.

There is nothing wrong with old soil, even though it is not nearly as good as the new container mix at sustaining new plant life. I start with fresh container mix in all of my pots and containers each spring, but I spread the existing soil from the pots over my garden and give them a quick rinse before adding the new stuff.

❧ FINAL WORDS

Encouraging diversity in our yards and on our balconies is entirely up to us. We can choose to manage our outdoor spaces strictly, planting only what we like, or we can relax and take the "managed chaos" approach. Either way, I encourage you to think carefully about the impact that you have on the biodiversity in your community through your gardening activities. Remember that the goal is to make a positive contribution to the desirable wildlife in your yard and beyond.

I choose the plants in my garden carefully. Aggressive plants, native or not, have no place in areas where I'm trying to keep diversity high. I need all plants to survive and thrive mutually.

Symbiosis in the garden is possible, but it takes time, some experimenting from year to year, and patience. No matter the size of space you have to garden in, you can create diversity. Consider joining a community group or taking part in the art of community gardening.

Chapter 3 will introduce this idea of gardening in a communal space and the benefits not only to yourself but to your community (human and non-). It will delve into the importance of supporting the local farm community. And give you some insight into managing a community plot in an efficient manner. Who knows, maybe you'll even want to set up your own for your community by the end of the chapter!

The praying mantis is → not native to Canada but provides a helpful set of chompers in the Canadian garden where insect pests are a concern.

Joe-pye weed and yellow coneflowers (*Rudbeckia lacinata*). →

THE COMMUNITY
GARDEN

CHAPTER THREE

I believe that there are two kinds of people in this world: those who love the experience of gardening, and the others, who enjoy observing gardens from the comfort of a bench or chair, content to let others do the work.

The idea of a shared communal space where nearby residents with limited green space of their own can come together, work the land, and produce a crop is not a new concept. First established in Europe as early as 1819, the practice of community gardening came over to North America sometime around 1890.

Gardening in public spaces has a rise and fall pattern. When times are good, people are less likely to garden for food; when economic times are difficult, we revert to growing our own. According to Amelia Garrett and Michael Leeds, the Depression of 1893, the First World War (1914–18), the Great Depression (1929–39), and the Second World War (1939–45) saw increases in urban community gardens and allotment plots.

By the end of the Second World War, 20 million "Victory Gardens" were providing 40 percent of the vegetables in America. Today, more than three million community gardens are being worked throughout North America. And while that number may seem significantly smaller than the 20 million during the Second World War, remember that our access to public space has dwindled greatly with urbanization.

Canadians want to garden. Despite the urbanization that has taken over much of Canada's previously open spaces, urbanites want to grow their own food. Many others want to grow food for those who are unable to afford it for themselves.

Today, North America is home to 42 million food gardens, and that number is increasing despite the decreasing size of the average yard. It is not uncommon for community gardens and allotment plots to have long waiting lists, attesting to the fact that their popularity is on the rise. Supply simply cannot keep up with demand. In a way, that's a good thing: we are changing, for the better.

This chapter provides the basics for building community and allotment gardens: what they are, how to best use the space, and how to go about acquiring a plot or starting your own. I talk about the numerous benefits brought to individual people and communities through the development of a communal garden plot and give you an inside look at community gardens across Canada.

The future of gardening is here: in our parks, on vacant lots, beside our workplaces and schools, on private and public land. The best part? We're all gardening together.

Public food gardening comes in many shapes and sizes. There are no set definitions for these terms, so I have provided you with my view. A view that is a combination of my own experience and various definitions that I have learned about over the years while researching for many newspaper articles on the subject.

Community Garden

A piece of private or public land that has been purposely converted for use as a garden. The gardens, food or otherwise, are maintained by volunteers. The produce (if that is the garden's function) is divided up amongst the volunteers or donated to local charities. All volunteers work together toward a common goal on the plot of land. Community gardens can also be broken into plots with each plot given to a family, group, or individual.

Allotment Garden

A piece of private or public land subdivided into smaller plots for the purpose of gardening (usually food, but it doesn't have to be). Each plot is rented and maintained by an individual, family, or small group of people. The produce grown in each plot belongs to the tenant and is his or hers to do with as they please, within the confines of the bylaws of the garden or the local municipality. Often allotment gardeners will share food with one another. Some use their plot to grow food for themselves and others use the plot to grow food that will be donated. Others use their plot as a "getaway" or retreat. Normally there are fees associated with allotment plots and they are generally larger than a community garden plot. For the purposes of this book, I'm not going to distinguish between community and allotment gardens as the terms are often used interchangeably.

Crabapple trees in bloom at Lauritzen Gardens at Omaha, Nebraska. →

Public Garden

Gardens located on public land and maintained by paid professionals. They are usually combinations of annuals and perennials put in place purely for aesthetic value. Access is free and attendance is encouraged with the placement of park benches and large shade trees.

Street/Container Gardens

These are window boxes or planters that are used to enhance the appearance of a street or community. Again, these are maintained by paid professionals, shop owners, or volunteers who put them in place to liven up the sidewalk.

Guerrilla Garden

This is a tricky one. Guerrilla gardens are not planted with permission from landowners or local government authorities, hence the name. Some guerrilla gardeners prefer using "seed bombs" — a mixture of clay (or other substrate) and seeds, which is thrown into areas they believe need to be enhanced by the presence of flowers. Seed bombs are rarely effective, however, and in some places, guerrilla gardening is illegal and may be deemed as vandalism or trespassing. Truth is, if you ask nicely, there's a good chance the owner of the land won't mind you putting plants in an abandoned area or somewhere that could use an aesthetic makeover. I know of some "guerilla gardeners" in Toronto who are ignored by City officials despite the fact that they are breaking the law. These same municipal officials will, from time to time, show up on site with free popsicles for the gardeners. Go figure.

In my opinion, you don't have to be the one providing all of the grunt work to enjoy the benefits of gardening. Just being around flowers, trees, and greenery has numerous positive health benefits. We know from statistics that urban (and suburban!) public gardens provide all of the health and wellness benefits that gardening on your own real estate does, with the added benefit of enjoying the social aspects associated with gardening as a community.

THE BENEFITS OF GARDENING TOGETHER

Scientific research has established beyond any doubt that gardening is good for you. From your mental to your physical health, gardening has been shown over and over to be a low-impact, highly beneficial form of exercise. Gardening in a public space with other people provides further benefits to the individual gardener and to the community as a whole.

Healthy Body

As I get older, I am realizing how important physical activity is. Not just for my heart and muscles, but for my sanity. Gardening is perhaps the most useful distraction from the phone, computer, and everything else that pulls at me during the day. My garden is my sanctuary.

Where my heart and muscles are concerned, gardening is my go-to activity for three-quarters of the year. Weeding, hoeing, planting, digging, mulching, and sometimes taking walks through my own garden and those of others provides me with more than the government recommended half-hour of exercise a day. And it's fun!

Studies have shown that people who garden are more likely to have healthy BMIs (body mass indices), fewer body pains, lower blood pressure, improved flexibility, and stronger muscles. If they have food gardens, they are more likely to eat healthier, too. Your partner and your children also benefit from having a gardener in the family. Generally speaking, it has been found that the whole family eats more vegetables and fruits when someone grows food than if no one in the family does. I like to think gardening has a radiating positive effect.

↑ Eating healthy veggies can be fun and nutritious.

For the kids, getting out into a public garden, whether it's one they are helping in or just a public space where they can run around, means they get to stretch their legs and exercise their bodies. As kids get older and become more involved in the act of planting, weeding, and maintaining a garden, they learn to appreciate the work that goes into creating, building, and sustaining the space. They continue the physical activity associated with gardening while building social, organizational, and time-management skills. It has been shown that they still eat better (more fruits and veggies) than those who don't garden at all and they have a greater understanding of healthy eating.

Healthy Mind

Gardening has been used in the past and present as a therapeutic tool. It has been proven that hospitalized patients suffering from similar problems will heal faster when placed in a room that looks out onto a garden or even at a tree. People who suffer from depression and anxiety are said to show signs of improvement quicker when given gardening tasks to complete. Among participants in garden therapy studies, the most commonly reported "symptom" of gardening is stress relief.

Stress is a funny thing. It not only affects your mental health, but it takes its toll on the body, as well. Gardening has been shown to reduce perceived stress, which in turn reduces blood pressure and the occurrence of ulcers, improves cardiovascular health, improves focus, and creates a sense of calm. For kids, studies have shown that time outdoors in parks, nature reserves, or gardens fosters a buffer of resilience against stress and the agents that cause stress. The book *Last Child in the Woods* quantifies many of the maladies associated with the disconnection between children and the world of nature.

Gardening for food, in particular, may help overcome the stress that comes with affording healthy food. In several studies, participants with lower-than-average household incomes reported that growing their own food reduced the stress and anxiety brought about by not being able to purchase adequate amounts of healthy food to feed their families.

Gardening at home, on a patio, or in a backyard provides a measure of mental health stimuli. Being outside, working the soil with your hands, watching plants grow from seed, and weeding produces a calm feeling few other activities can provide. Now take that beneficial activity and share it with other like-minded individuals. The social aspect of community gardening amplifies the mental benefits of the experience.

Community gardens are growing more than flowers and vegetables. They are growing positive attitudes, a place where people of all ages, genders, races, and backgrounds can come together and feel safe. They provide places where individuals can try something new with the help of others to guide them, find motivation and confidence in other areas of their life, and reflect and relax.

Healthy Communities

When we garden in public spaces in the company of others, we open ourselves up for communication and social interaction (might sound scary, but it's really not). We bring ourselves closer to those who are engaging in a similar activity and it becomes easier to start a discussion, increasing the potential for new friendships.

In community and allotment gardens, the sharing of seeds, tools, and knowledge serve to increase relationships between neighbours. I find it strange that we live so close together these days, yet interact with so few of our neighbours. Many people don't engage in conversations with strangers in day-to-day life because they don't know how to begin. Community gardening provides a starting point, a common goal, and a mutual interest.

I claim that gardening cures shyness: put the shyest gardener in a room with strangers who also enjoy gardening and sooner or later conversation erupts. A common interest always encourages discussion; gardening is perhaps the strongest motivator for conversation and debate. To test this theory, try asking a stranger who gardens what they think of the weather. What may be deemed as small talk with the in-laws is a serious topic of conversation where gardeners are concerned.

Public gardens are connected with increased neighbour awareness (we see our neighbours as friends and not strangers), reduced vandalism

RECOVERYPARK

RecoveryPark is a one-of-a-kind place. It's difficult to pick just a few words to describe it because it is unique in all aspects. The organization began back in 2010 with the overall goal to improve the lives of those living in Detroit, provide fresh, healthy food to local businesses, and bring awareness to environmental stewardship in a town that is not really known for any of those things.

The not-for-profit business is broken up into three separate strategies: RecoveryPark Farms, RecoveryPark Fisheries, and RecoveryPark Foods. In 2014, RecoveryPark Farms grew more than 25 types of food. The food went to local restaurants owners, who pay a premium price for the locally grown food.

The food is grown to a high standard, with the environment a high priority. Water is recycled, energy use is considered on all levels, and rather than resorting to chemical control for every issue, biological pest control is employed.

Those who are running the project foresee a 40-acre park where community members are welcome to walk in and learn about the project; the entire project supplying thousands of jobs to local Detroit residents.

Did I mention that the work is completed, in part, by recovering addicts, those who have recently been released from prison, and others who have barriers to employment? Founder Gary Wozniak is a former addict himself, having spent a number of years in prison. Upon release, he decided to make a difference in a community he saw struggling. Recovery Park aims to not only beautify the city but provide meaningful work for those who are having difficulties finding it.

(especially when kids are involved in the gardening), an increased sense of pride and satisfaction with community, social tolerance with respect to age, race, gender, and physical differences, and individual empowerment within the community. All of these benefits stem directly from having access to public gardens and encouraging continuous engagement in public gardening.

The urge to bring communities together under the common interest of gardening is so strong here in Canada that it has bred a giant organization that stretches across the country. Communities in Bloom started out as an idea based on the very premise that gardens add beauty, demonstrate civic pride, and help to build communities. Many participants in studies related to the effects of community gardens on the community itself reported feeling safer within their community. That feeling comes from knowing your neighbours, seeing less vandalism and fewer instances of drug use on the streets, and a sense of having eyes and ears watching out for you while you do the same for others. In the end, the community is brought closer together, physically and socially.

Canada

Communities in Bloom
People, Plants and Pride
...Growing Together

® **Collectivités en fleurs**
Citoyens et espaces verts en harmonie
...une société florissante

A COMMON GOAL

Community gardens don't happen overnight. For a garden to be successful, whether it is an open public space, a community garden, or an allotment plot, the community needs to come together, working toward a common goal. Goals for the garden should be detailed and specific, as each project will have different variables to juggle. Are you a leader in your community who can help to make this happen? Or the one to perpetuate a quality experience that others started before you? If not, do you know someone who can carry this torch? Don't wait for politicians to make this happen. In my experience, the most successful community gardening experiences are born from grassroots sources.

The benefits of community gardening are vast and cross all cultural, age, and gender barriers. Gardeners who grow food want to share their bounty, want to show you their plot, want to ask questions and share their experiences, too. Perhaps the greatest advantage of public gardens is that everyone benefits, even those who are not doing any actual gardening. The joy I've seen on the face of an observer, whether they are knowledgeable about the project or just passing through, is motivation to continue, to improve, and to engage others. Many see these gardens as extensions of their own: adding to the value of the community.

Gardening on public land is inherently different than gardening on real estate that belongs to you. The fundamental aspects of gardening are the same (how deep to plant, how much sun each plant needs), but there are some aspects that need to be given particular attention. In the next section, I will give you some pointers on how to make efficient use of the space you are given and a few other things you need to think about before doing any planting.

Using Your Plot Wisely

How do you get the greatest productivity, or colour, from a community garden? It is a fair question. Here are some pointers on how to use your allocated space efficiently. For practical information, I will refer you back to Chapter 1, where I outlined in greater detail the cultural information about growing plants, like plant spacing and the best plants for use in small spaces.

Here is an example of → a basic sketch of a plot and the surrounding features. Don't get too hung up on your artistic abilities. It should be simple and easy to understand.

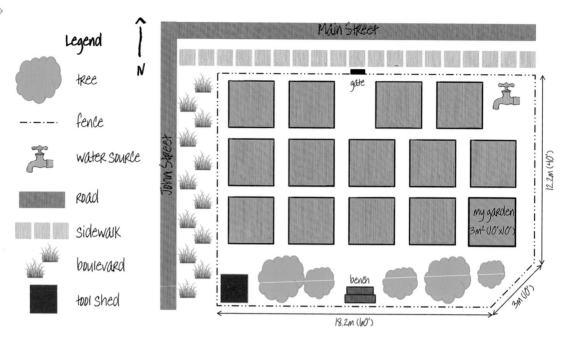

Legend

🌳 tree

— ∙ — ∙ — fence

🚰 water source

▬ road

▭▭▭ sidewalk

🌾 boulevard

◼ tool shed

Main Street

N

John Street

gate

my garden
3m² (10'x10')

bench

12.2m (40')

3m (10')

18.2m (60')

Considering Your Plot Size

It doesn't matter if you pay to rent a plot or use it for free, the size of your plot and your soil conditions will determine what you *can* grow. Your personal preferences will determine what you *should* grow. I am assuming that your plot is located in full sun or with at least six hours per day of sunshine. Otherwise, you will have trouble growing most herbs and vegetables.

First, I recommend that you draw a sketch of the plot and the surrounding features. Include a compass, the location of water sources, trees or buildings that may cast shade on your plot, and, of course, the plot itself with measurements included. No need to be a natural artist, just sketch your plot out roughly. Then make a list of what you like to eat. For me, tomatoes are a must.

Next, organize your plot. One of the easiest ways to do this is to divide your plot into

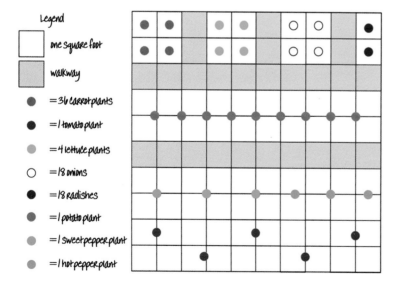

Legend

▢ one square foot

▨ walkway

● = 36 carrot plants

● = 1 tomato plant

● = 4 lettuce plants

○ = 18 onions

● = 18 radishes

● = 1 potato plant

● = 1 sweet pepper plant

● = 1 hot pepper plant

↑ Plot out the number of seeds or plants you will need to fill each section.

square-foot sections. Use the table on pages 24–25 to determine how much of each vegetable you can plant in one square foot. Helpful information on the back of seed packages or on plant tags will get you started.

Keep in mind that some vegetables are "space pigs." For example, I do not recommend growing corn or any of the squashes, including pumpkins, if you are "square-foot gardening." They just take up too much real estate.

Create a new sketch, a top view of your plot, indicating the placement of each of the vegetables/fruits you would like to grow. Make a list of the number of seeds or plants you will need to fill each section. The following should be considered when choosing your crops:

Soil Condition

Consider the soil's quality. Is the soil in good shape? Is it loamy, soft, and not compacted? Is there potential for the soil to be contaminated? If so, discuss the potential with a professional. Your local garden retailer or bulk-soil supplier may be helpful. Most often, a well-established community or allotment plot will have quality soil in place. Be sure to add generous quantities of compost to it each season to enhance the quality and to ensure that you will enjoy a healthy crop. The garden organizers may even do this each year but it will depend on the garden. See page 41 for details on soil prep.

Buy your garden seeds ahead of time as some varieties sell out quickly when the season gets started. Purchase your transplants as close to planting day as possible. Store transplants on the north side of a building or in a shed or garage when frost is threatened.

If you are starting seeds at home for transplanting, consider the time needed for each plant to mature. I start my tomatoes in mid March and my mesclun lettuce a few weeks after for my Zone 5 garden.

Plant according to the type of vegetable/fruit. Tomatoes cannot withstand a frost but broccoli can. In Canada, we often say that the long weekend in May is the weekend to plant. I recommend that you check my list of first frost-free dates (pages 136–38). In my Zone 5 location, I do not plant out frost-tender plants until May 24 (not necessarily the holiday weekend).

Shade can have a negative effect on plants that require lots of sun. Here you can see how the trees shade the corn, causing obvious undulating crop heights. ↓

FROST-FREE DATES

City	Province	Growing Season (Length in Days)	Last Frost Spring	First Frost Fall
Athabasca	AB	88	June 1	August 29
Calgary	AB	114	May 23	September 15
Edmonton	AB	138	May 7	September 23
Elk Point	AB	92	June 1	September 1
Grande Prairie	AB	117	May 18	September 13
Lethbridge	AB	123	May 17	September 18
Medicine Hat	AB	128	May 16	September 22
Peace River	AB	99	May 26	September 3
Red Deer	AB	106	May 25	September 9
Vegreville	AB	85	June 5	August 29
Vermilion	AB	107	May 25	September 9
Abbotsford	BC	177	April 24	October 18
Chilliwack	BC	216	April 6	November 9
Dawson Creek	BC	84	June 5	August 29
Kamloops	BC	156	May 1	October 5
Kelowna	BC	156	May 4	October 8
Nanaimo	BC	171	April 28	October 17
Nelson	BC	159	May 4	October 13
Port Alberni	BC	159	May 8	October 15
Prince George	BC	91	June 4	September 3
Prince Rupert	BC	156	May 9	October 13
Terrace	BC	165	May 5	October 17
Vancouver	BC	221	March 28	November 5
Vernon	BC	159	April 28	October 4
Victoria	BC	200	April 19	November 5
Brandon	MB	105	May 27	September 10
Lynn Lake	MB	89	June 8	September 6
The Pas	MB	112	May 27	September 17

FROST-FREE DATES

City	Province	Growing Season (Length in Days)	Last Frost Spring	First Frost Fall
Thompson	MB	61	June 15	August 16
Winnipeg	MB	119	May 25	September 22
Bathurst	NB	129	May 19	September 26
Edmundston	NB	112	May 28	September 18
Fredericton	NB	124	May 20	September 22
Grand Falls	NB	123	May 24	September 24
Moncton	NB	125	May 24	September 27
Saint John	NB	139	May 18	October 4
Corner Brook	NL	142	May 22	October 12
Grand Falls	NL	115	June 2	September 26
St. John's	NL	131	June 2	October 12
Halifax	NS	166	May 6	October 20
Kentville	NS	141	May 16	October 5
Shelburne	NS	138	May 14	September 29
Sydney	NS	141	May 24	October 13
Truro	NS	113	May 30	September 21
Yarmouth	NS	169	May 1	October 18
Aklavik	NWT	76	June 13	August 31
Fort Simpson	NWT	81	June 3	August 24
Yellowknife	NWT	110	May 27	September 15
Barrie	ON	112	May 26	September 16
Hamilton	ON	168	Apr. 29	October 15
Kapuskasing	ON	87	June 12	September 8
Kingston	ON	160	May 2	October 10
Kitchener	ON	139	May 11	September 29
London	ON	151	May 9	October 8
Ottawa	ON	151	May 6	October 5
Owen Sound	ON	155	May 12	October 15

City	Province	Growing Season (Length in Days)	Last Frost Spring	First Frost Fall

FROST-FREE DATES

City	Province	Growing Season (Length in Days)	Last Frost Spring	First Frost Fall
Parry Sound	ON	134	May 17	September 28
Peterborough	ON	124	May 18	September 20
Sudbury	ON	130	May 17	September 25
Thunder Bay	ON	105	June 1	September 15
Timmins	ON	89	June 8	September 6
Toronto	ON	149	May 9	October 6
Windsor	ON	179	April 25	October 22
Charlottetown	PEI	150	May 17	October 14
Summerside	PEI	162	May 9	October 19
Tignish	PEI	138	May 23	October 9
Baie Comeau	QC	109	May 28	September 15
Chicoutimi	QC	133	May 17	September 30
Montreal	QC	156	May 3	October 7
Quebec	QC	139	May 13	September 29
Rimouski	QC	139	May 13	September 30
Sherbrooke	QC	100	June 1	September 10
Tadoussac	QC	141	May 13	October 2
Thetford Mines	QC	106	May 28	September 14
Trois-Rivières	QC	124	May 19	September 23
Moose Jaw	SK	120	May 20	September 18
North Battleford	SK	120	May 19	September 17
Prince Albert	SK	93	June 2	September 4
Regina	SK	111	May 21	September 10
Saskatoon	SK	116	May 21	September 15
Weyburn	SK	112	May 22	September 12
Yorkton	SK	110	May 23	September 11
Dawson City	YT	62	June 13	August 17
Watson Lake	YT	91	June 2	September 4

Harden off any plant starts you have. This process strengthens the plant and protects it from droughts, heavy winds, and cold snaps. See page 51 for the hardening off method I use for my plants.

Nurture your plants but don't overdo it: there is a fine line between watering properly and negligence. The most common mistake I see in gardening is watering too much. Some plants need more water than others but all will need a good deep watering every (sunny) day for about a week after planting to get them established. Of course, if it rains, don't water. As the season progresses, water when the top five centimetres of soil are dry. I use the "knuckle test" and push my finger up to my knuckle into the soil. When the soil is dry to my knuckle, I water deeply. Watering deeply encourages roots to grow downward in search of water and creates more drought-tolerant plants.

Weeding is a job that never ends, but it can be managed. After a couple seasons of weeding you will learn the rhythm of their growth cycles and know when to get out there to knock them down and when to relax and let them grow.

Fortunately, gardening in a small plot and planting close together leaves less room for weeds. Keep on top of it, ten minutes or less a day, and it won't become a burden down the road. Any weeds that do germinate won't live long enough to pull nutrients and water from your plant, leaving you with healthier plants that produce delicious edibles and colourful flowers. One of the advantages of a community garden is that you only need to observe when the experienced gardeners are hoeing down their weeds. That is your cue to do the same.

↑ A weeded versus an un-weeded allotment garden.

Community Garden Etiquette

When you garden on public land, there is a certain level of respect and courtesy you should extend toward the property and your neighbours. Even if you are paying to rent an allotment garden, you should still treat the area the way you would treat a public walking trail or park and leave it better than you found it.

Most community gardens will have rules that participants are asked to follow. These can vary from water usage to gardening times and everything in between. Before you start planting or doing anything with your plot, be sure you read and understand the rules. If you are unsure, ask. The rules are put in place to keep participants safe, the plots clean, and ensure that everyone is getting the most out of their experience.

Garden only in your own plot unless you have an agreement with another gardener. Don't put trimmings or other garden materials into another person's plot and return tools where you found them. Some community gardens have a community shed where tools are kept: return what you take, clean tools that you use, keep the area organized, and lock it up when you're finished. If your community garden doesn't have a composter, consider asking to have one installed. It will benefit every gardener and the soil will thank you as well as the plants that you grow in it.

Don't plant tall (or trellised) plants where they will shade out another garden; keep your plants within the specified guidelines (for example, avoid woody perennial plants in plots). Don't bring in other substrate: no gravel or sand; and don't leave large rocks in your plot. If you bring a pet, be sure it is leashed and kept under control at all times; clean up after your pet and don't let them wander into other people's plots. Here are some other factors to keep in mind:

Watering

Some plots charge for water use. And even if you are not charged, someone is. Water is never free and you should always be smart about it. Use the weather to judge when you should water your plot. If you have the option to use rain water, I encourage you to do it. Rain water is "oxygen charged," warm, and free. What's not to like?

Chemicals

If you live in an area where chemicals can be used to treat garden problems, consider your neighbouring gardeners before you go spraying willy-nilly. Most gardens do not allow the use of chemicals even if the province or territory has not outright banned them. If you are new to the garden, talk with

Posting an information plaque at your community garden can be a good way of advertising. You may wish to include fees on the plot or you may wish to direct prospective gardeners to a website where they can get more information, especially if fees are subject to change annually.

seasoned gardeners about their expectations when it comes to chemical spraying. Ask them what they use (if anything) and how it has worked. Their experience may save you time and money down the road.

Cleanup

Perhaps it goes without saying that cleaning up after yourself in a community or allotment garden is the courteous thing to do. But I said it anyway.

Organic Materials

It is not a good idea to throw organic waste directly into a garden. Banana peels and other kitchen or yard waste should be composted, where it will break down into humus and provide needed nutrients for the soil. Organic food waste can attract unwanted critters to the garden, composted organic food waste will not.

End of Season

At the end of the season, clean up and prep work for next season is essential. The degree of cleaning will depend on the stipulations of your agreement but will generally include removing dead plant material (to the compost, please!), pulling up spent vegetable plants, and disposing of weeds.

↑ Install a rain barrel or two to take advantage of the free water.

Most plots will have a disposal method (composter, boxed and put at the curb, etc.). You will also be required to pull up stakes, dispose of twine or other materials used to secure plants, and clean up the path around your plot. Basically, you are to leave it as you found it, only better. If the gardens are rototilled in the spring, a clear path to and from the gardens is essential.

A Final Note

Some community gardens or allotment plots have consistent group meetings. The people who put together the meetings are likely the same as those organizing the garden plots. I encourage you to attend at least some of these meetings. You will meet new people, re-acquaint yourself with gardening friends, and you might be surprised at what you learn while there!

Take pride in what you are doing, what you're growing, and the garden space as a whole. Keep the space clean and your attitude friendly. Go out of your way to pick up trash, talk with your plot neighbours, and spend a little extra time maintaining your plot than your contract stipulates. A little common courtesy and friendly behaviour goes a long way in establishing healthy relationships with those around you.

If you live in an area that doesn't have a community garden or allotment plot, why not organize one? Section four of this chapter will provide you with some general guidelines for starting a community garden, some ideas for advertising the plot, and some really great resources you shouldn't be without should you undertake this endeavour.

↑ Raised gardens provide the option of instantly planting in great quality soil.

 **STARTING A GARDEN**

Starting your own community garden or allotment plot may seem like a lot of work, but keep in mind that a garden like this is a group effort: you won't be tackling any of these tasks alone. There are a few important legal considerations to take into account, but they aren't overly complicated. Each city or municipality will have different rules and regulations regarding land use. Start by checking out the city's website. You may find exactly what you're looking for or you may not. You will definitely find contact information, though, and I encourage you to take advantage of this.

Step 1: Discuss Your Idea

If you are looking for a place to garden within your community, there's a good chance others are, too. Put up flyers, visit your neighbours, or put an ad in the paper (many local papers will offer free classifieds). Set up a meeting date and time at a local coffee shop, park, or other establishment you may have access to. Be sure to talk with your local municipal councillor or mayor: you might be surprised how helpful they can be in this process!

↑ Community garden.

An initial organizational meeting is a good time to delegate jobs and create your plan — the *who*, *what*, *when*, and *how* of a new community or allotment garden. You will need people to organize meetings, clean up the future plot, take minutes, etc. In essence, you are forming a committee, and in order to keep things running smoothly, each person should be in charge of certain tasks.

So, what should be on the agenda for that initial meeting? The first thing would be to decide whether a garden is needed, and if so, what type (vegetable, flower, public green space with gardens interspersed throughout). Discuss garden knowledge and get to know each member of the group. If anyone has ideas for garden location, take note of them. Define your idea of the project and open it up to others. Most importantly, keep the meeting casual: people will potentially be working fairly closely with one another on the project. Feel comfortable delegating tasks and try to be inclusive of all members of the group, regardless of their experience level.

Step 2: Establish Connections

A community garden needs two very basic things: people and land. You have found the people (or some of them), who are hopefully like-minded and with some enthusiasm for the project. For sources of land, talk with your fellow gardeners and local politicians and staff in your municipality. I can only hope that someone with authority and knowledge will want to help you with your public gardening endeavour. What, after all, is not to like about it?

Garden clubs and horticultural societies are an excellent source of information, inspiration, experience, and willing volunteers for your new public garden. Exhaust all of your resources: neighbouring community gardening groups, libraries, Internet resources, local horticultural societies, garden groups, etc.

Step 3: Choose Your Site

A community garden or allotment plot should be easily accessible, safe and well-lit, receive full sun, and have access to plenty of clean water. Good soil is not necessarily a factor, as most often soil is brought in to fill individual raised beds.

Step 4: Develop a Proposal

Using the information you already have, begin a proposal for your project. The proposal will be useful for you to present down the road when you ask for funding or when you approach a landowner, but for now it will be useful for you to really understand your project. Refer to the Resources section at the back of this book for a full organized proposal template. Here are the basics. Your proposal should include the following topics:

- What you propose to do
- Why the community needs this garden
- How you will achieve your goal
- Breakdown of expenses
- How you plan to get funding
- Timeline of events and completion
- Challenges you anticipate
- Short member bios

Step 5: Discuss Funding

If you and your group are funding the project yourselves, then you can skip this section. In all likelihood, though, you are not funding it yourselves and you will need sponsors. Discuss amongst the group who may have connections to someone willing to sponsor your project. Approach them with the proposal you have already written. Consider local government, lottery funds, businesses (especially any that might benefit directly from the gardening activity in your community),

service clubs, horticultural societies, veterans associations, etc.

Supporting a local food bank by providing some or all of the produce generated from your local food garden is a sure way of getting the local community on board. Many patrons and supporters of food banks are predisposed to helping you get your garden up and running. There is a groundswell of interest in Canada when it comes to providing locally produced food to people who otherwise cannot afford it.

Consider holding fundraising events in the community: offer to clean leaves in a yard for a minimum sponsor of X amount of dollars put toward the community garden. Be sure to explain the end goal of the garden and that 100 percent of the funds will go toward its start-up and maintenance. This can be a yearly event, or you may find that your sponsors grow in number as the garden gains momentum.

Money raised from fundraising in addition to fees collected from garden users can provide enough income to sustain a public gardening scheme from year to year. "Allotment" gardening is a good way to ensure those who are renting the plots are going to take care of them. The allotment

A worthy endeavour. This Calgary public food garden donates 100 percent of all food grown to the local food bank. ↑

organization only allows users back the following year if they act responsibly.

Sponsoring doesn't have to be financial. You may want to approach a retailer of garden tools and ask for a donation or discount on the products you need (trowels, rakes, hoes, etc.); or you may want to solicit the help of someone in the community who can build the raised beds. Be creative, and remember the number one rule of fundraising: you cannot say *thank you* too many times!

Step 6: Identify the Site Owner

Even public space is owned by someone. Do some digging and find out who owns the site you've chosen as your primary option. The local municipal councillor is a great resource for this type of information. Contact the owner with your idea. If they are interested in the project, discuss leasing options or if they would be willing to let you garden in return for keeping the area clean and maintained. You'd be surprised at how many people would rather see their land being put to use for the public good.

If your idea is rejected by a landowner, do not be discouraged. Keep asking until you get the answer that you are looking for. I remember hearing Marnie McBean, the three-time gold medal Olympic rower for Canada, speak at a Home Hardware conference. She said that the best news she ever received from a coach was that she would lose 50 times before she would win a race. She found that so encouraging because it meant that every time she lost a race she was one race closer to winning. THAT is the attitude you need when asking for favours. Keep counting … 50, 49, 48 …

Once your site has been chosen and you've been given the go-ahead, address any legal considerations the landowner may have and keep the owner informed throughout the process. Your local municipality may have a "boiler plate" agreement that you can use for this purpose. Make sure the landowner understands your plan and your course of action. Remember, you are working on someone else's property.

Remember to ask about water: whether it is already hooked up or if it can be. A community garden, especially one whose purpose is to grow vegetables, will not function well without easy water access, and installing a new access point can cost a pretty penny.

Also, plan on improving the existing soil, no matter how good it is. Seek the advice of a professional to be sure that the soil is well-prepared for planting come spring.

Step 7: Organize the Space

Now that you've secured a location, it's time to think about how you want it set up. Go back to your proposal and review your goals. Have they changed? Note the water source and if there isn't one, you will need to put one in.

Consider kids in your plan and set aside a garden for them. If you have a school in the area, perhaps offer that garden as a "school garden." It will depend on the principal and teachers, but you could offer it to anyone in the school who is interested or you could approach a certain grade and offer them the space each year with the idea that the kids come into the garden to learn how to grow vegetables or flowers. Note that the number one reason why school gardens fail is that they are not properly tended to over the summer/vacation months.

Will you have a communal garden shed located on the property to hold tools and hoses? How many raised beds can you fit comfortably within the space? Will the garden need a fence and gate? Be sure to review the plan with the landowner if you have made changes they haven't seen.

One obvious but often overlooked issue is that of washrooms. Make sure you have a plan and be sure to offer a place where people can wash their hands, even if it is under a rain barrel.

Step 8: Set Guidelines

I've already mentioned some rules set out by other community gardens earlier in this chapter, and it's in your best interest to draw up a set of guidelines of your own that pertain to your particular garden. You want people to feel welcome and comfortable working there but you also want them to feel safe and to give them a sense of structure. Guidelines also help them understand their responsibilities as garden plot renters. In the Resource section for Chapter 3, I have provided a sample template you can follow when structuring your garden's rules and regulations.

Step 9: Get to Work

Once the plans have been drawn up, the money and resources collected or sourced, and space secured for use, it's time to start putting it all together. Begin by cleaning up debris and garbage: this part will vary greatly with each site. You may have to make a trip to the dump, or, if it's not very much, it can be bagged and thrown out with household waste.

At this point, you may have locals stop and ask questions. They will see you and your volunteers working away, cleaning and prepping the site, and they will be interested. Give them information if they ask. It may even be worthwhile to print off a half-page information sheet about the project and who to contact should they be interested in renting a plot. Or you could create a web page that is

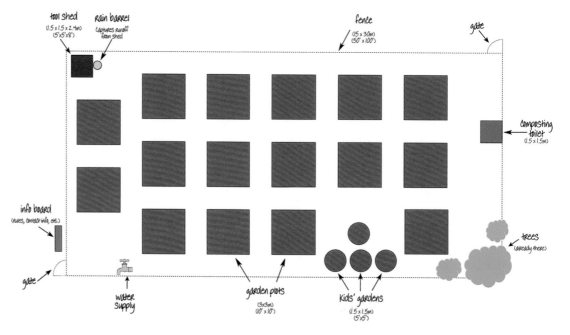

↑ A well-thought-out garden plan is essential. Be sure to review your plan with the landowner.

linked from the municipality and/or local garden or horticultural clubs' sites.

Build your planting boxes at least 30 centimetres deep to accommodate deeper-rooted crops, and those like carrots and potatoes whose roots are what you're after, place them appropriately, and fill with soil. Consider fencing the gardens for security reasons. Plan to put up a sign with the name of your garden and some rules of "common courtesy." Add contact information so that visitors can learn more about the project.

This part of the process will take some time, especially if you want to do it right (and you do).

Step 10: Advertising

Once your garden is ready to be planted up, it's time to solicit members. You may have filled your spaces in the time it took you to prepare the space, or you may have spots left. Those who came out to the first meeting and have been helping and volunteering their time throughout the process are likely interested in a plot, so be sure to accommodate them first.

Contact local radio stations, TV stations, and newspapers that may be interested in a story about your garden. This is a way to get the information out there and let people know what you

↑ Sooke community garden, Vancouver Island.

have to offer. Hold a public information session in the garden, asking your gardening group to spread the word. Libraries and other public buildings often have public notice boards and local garden clubs may be willing to put out the word as well. Let any sponsors know that spaces are available and encourage them to communicate the message through their client/vendor networks.

Each community and garden is different. It's up to you to determine the best way to reach the appropriate audience.

Step 11: Garden

I suggest you throw a garden party where community gardeners can get to know one another. Tour them around the space, designate plots, and go over the rules while everybody is in attendance to ensure they all understand. If you are planning to have a children's plot for the gardeners' children or a local school, invite them, too.

During this info session, be sure to answer any questions. Find out who has previous gardening experience and who will need assistance. Offer learning sessions for those who are interested and teach them about square-foot gardening (see page 24 for more information). But, above all, have fun! Bringing strangers together under the common theme of the gardening experience is a great opportunity to make friends and build communities.

Consider a "buddy system" for new gardeners, and don't miss the opportunity to celebrate the harvest each fall with a special dinner/barbecue/social evening. The key is that you are celebrating all that you have achieved as a group.

Step 12: Foster Community

Community gardens are about gardening and social interaction. To a degree, gardeners will interact with one another on a daily basis, but you can facilitate interaction by holding community gatherings. Monthly meetings that are convenient for most members can be used as purely a social experience or you can make it a multi-purpose social and learning session. Ask gardeners to bring a friend, neighbour, or relative. Hold a weekend session for kids, with games where prizes consist of seeds or pre-started seedlings. Organize a planting lesson during the session and make sure everyone leaves with something. Teach them about beneficial insects (a number are discussed in Chapter 1), pollinators, and that food doesn't start in a grocery store.

Consider a suggestion box in your garden (maybe in the tool shed?) and be sure to open it and respond regularly.

↑ A firm push on the soil helps to establish the plant.

✿ FINAL WORDS

Starting your own community gardening space is a bit of work, but just as with anything in life, working hard comes with big rewards. Not only will you have secured a place for you to garden and grow the vegetables and flowers you would have otherwise not been able to, but you have done the same for others in the community.

By keeping the rules simple and fair, engaging children with their own space, and encouraging social interaction, you will have built trust between fellow community members and helped in no small way to enhance life for all in your community. It's highly likely that you will have started friendships that will continue beyond the garden and spread farther into the community. Sometimes people just need a reason to come together, and you will have an opportunity to provide the best reasons of all: fresh air, physical activity, social interaction, and healthy food. Wow!

Community gardening is more than growing vegetables. A good deal of work goes into the creation and upkeep of a publicly gardened space,

and it doesn't just happen overnight. The planning alone before the growing even begins is enough to scare some people away.

Truth is, we need gardeners in our communities and we need community gardens. We need to spread the word that gardening doesn't have to be a solitary hobby. We can garden together, garden with a purpose, and make use of space that is otherwise underutilized.

I hope that you are inspired to get out into your community and start up or volunteer at a community garden. As you become involved in public allotment or community gardens, you will gain an appreciation for the blooms you see in the streets, the green spaces where your children play, and the beds filled with fresh veggies in your community. Maybe you didn't notice these things before; I bet you will now.

The next chapter delves into the world of gardening with children. Kids are naturally inclined to play outdoors, get their hands and knees dirty, and ask a lot of questions. I hope to provide you with a little insight into how to engage children where gardening is concerned and give you some ideas for projects that kids of any age can participate in.

THE LEARNING
GARDEN

CHAPTER FOUR

My very first memory of a gardening experience was when I was about four years old (no one knows for sure). My family had several rows of vegetables in the ground on the "other side of the back fence" in a hydro right-of-way.

One fine Saturday morning my dad took my two sisters, my brother, and me out to "help" him in the garden. He showed me a weed and how to pull it while standing at one end of a long row of potatoes. They were gorgeous, big plants with deep green leaves and white flowers. He said, "Pull the weeds starting here and let me know when you get to the end of the row."

I did as I was told, and when I arrived at the end of the row, I pulled out the last weed and held the most beautiful (albeit small) potato in the air, "Hey, Dad, is this a weed?"

I will never forget the look on his face at that very moment. Did he want to kill me or just hope that I would never become a career gardener as he was? I will never know. But I know one thing for sure: where gardening is concerned, there is no such thing as "failure," only composting opportunities.

Kids and adults alike have this in common: we need to know that there is a place where we can push the envelope, take a risk, and know that the consequences will never amount to more than a dead plant or two. Which, in the overall scheme of things, is nothing.

I have four kids: four great kids who grew up to be as different from one another as they are from me. Not that that's a bad thing; in fact, I'm very happy with the wonderful people they've become, even though only one of them has picked up the trowel and become a professional gardener. Heather is actually a Landscape Architect and, oddly enough, the only kid that we named after a plant. Go figure.

When they were younger, Mary and I encouraged outdoor activities. I would spend time gardening and they would spend their time digging through the dirt and in the sandbox (as kids are wont to do). Sometimes we would root around in the soil together: they would dig it up for me as I planted a new perennial. They didn't really know they were gardening at the time.

As they got older, gardening activities became something with a purpose; taking raw material from the kitchen out to the compost pile was a job that each of them had from time to time while growing up.

They may not share my obsession with gardening, but, to an extent, all of them have learned and earned an appreciation for nature and its role in our world.

🍁 LEARNING FROM NATURE

Gardening with kids is a great way to spend time together and to create connections beyond the human-to-human contact they receive on a daily basis. It inspires curiosity and fosters respect, generosity, and kindness. If you teach them the value of something as small as an ant, and you teach them to respect life that is physically smaller than they are, that knowledge extends beyond the garden. They begin to see value in other people and in themselves.

The purpose of this chapter is to teach you how to teach your children the value of the gardening experience. Note that I did not say "teach them how to garden." Those of us that choose this pastime as a hobby or a career are always learning. That is a huge part of the attraction to it. In this regard, we have something in common with kids: we are always learning as long as we are taking risks and trying new things. We are experimenting every day that we are out there and learning in the laboratory that we call "the garden."

↑ Let's play in the dirt again!

Learning how to garden is reasonably straightforward. Ask a neighbour with a good-looking lawn and garden how to do it and you will likely end up with more information than you bargained for. The part that takes more effort is our appreciation for the time that we invest in our gardens. There is value in there somewhere and it will be different for each gardener.

If you are new to gardening, teaching the concepts to someone else, no matter their age, may seem daunting. If you are a seasoned gardener, but not sure how to teach someone else, it can be just as tough to get started. I will provide a few activities for you to do with your kids, no matter their age. And once you get the hang of it, I encourage you to go beyond the scope of this chapter and engage them in activities beyond gardening: think bigger — ecosystems, building insect hotels, bioswales, hiking trails, exploring forests. Learn with them, and when they ask questions you don't know the answer to, find the answers together.

↑ Getting out on hiking trails is a great way for kids to explore nature.

✿ THE IMPORTANCE OF ENGAGING THE YOUNGER GENERATION

Gardening is sometimes seen as an activity for retirees: those who have plenty of time to just muck about out of doors. There is no doubt that seniors derive as many benefits from digging, weeding, and generally growing things in the garden as the rest of us do. Truth is, every generation can, and should, get involved. There's something about playing in the dirt that puts you in touch with nature and instills values like no other activity can.

In Chapter 3, we talked about the benefits of gardening on the lives of children. Not only does it encourage healthy eating, it fosters discipline and respect. Who doesn't want that for their kids? In urban cities, where crime is higher and temptation runs around every corner, the garden can be a positive escape. As our kids turn into teens and then move into their adult years, they will carry with them these skills and a deeper appreciation for the world of nature that surrounds us. The results can be very positive and will last a lifetime.

When we teach our children to garden, and to appreciate gardening, we are ensuring a future where trees, homegrown vegetables, curbside flower beds, and balcony gardens are the norm. We instill a love for these features in our neighbourhoods and raise kids who are proud to say they can garden.

In all honesty, gardening does not have an exclusive hold on the benefits of the activity. Walking outdoors, through parks and nature reserves, attending free learning sessions at your local wildlife centre, or visiting a local pond to see the tadpoles in the spring all foster imagination and curiosity. Our goal as adults is to keep that curiosity going. Too often we see kids hit a wall at a certain age, usually around grade six, where it's not "cool" to show an interest in growing plants any more.

Fortunately, one of the trends that I see developing across the country is the installation of gardens in schools, where gardening is either an actual class or an extracurricular activity. The benefits that stem from programs like these are enormous. With every seed sown and plant nurtured comes a deeper appreciation for where it came from and what it represents. In time a child will learn that a flower is not created exclusively for our enjoyment and use, but to attract pollinators in an effort for the plant to reproduce. Fruit is not for our consumption exclusively, but was designed in nature to protect and feed seeds as they journey toward maturity and perhaps the germination of a new generation of plants.

I think all of us want to live in a world filled with people who are inclined to plant just one more flower, grow an extra row of vegetables for a neighbour in need, or lend a helping green thumb on a sunny afternoon. Our kids will be those people if we encourage these activities early. There are so many ways we can get our kids to garden and be outside (and enjoy it). And here's a little story that was my real inspiration to write this chapter. It was a real eye-opener for me. Maybe it will be for you, too.

Knowing they did it themselves gives children a sense of pride. ↑

The Game Changer

While interviewing a young child on his obsession with being indoors, Richard Louv leaned in toward the young lad and asked, "What is it about being indoors that you find so appealing?"

"That's where the electrical outlets are," was his reply.

It was on that day in 2004 that Mr. Louv decided that he would write a book that explores the importance of nature in the lives of young people. *Last Child in the Woods: Saving Our Children from Nature Deficit Disorder* was published in 2005 and won the Audubon Medal. Since then, many thousands of people have added the expression "nature deficit disorder" to their lexicon. And the rest is history.

While it has been more than a decade since Louv first published his landmark book, kids continue to sequester themselves indoors, usually as near to a computer or some electronic gadget as possible. I read recently that we are at risk of developing permanently hunched backs from constantly looking down at our electronic handheld devices.

While all of this raises the question "What has this world come to?" I have another: "What can we do to reverse this trend?" You see, I believe that we can change this episode in our history by helping kids discover the wonders of the natural world by exposing them to fun and interesting components of it, beginning right in their own backyards (and balconies). This next story is the exact opposite of the one above. It proves that it is, indeed, possible in this day and age to send our kids outside for the day and call them back in for dinner.

↑ Discovering the natural world.

The Ultimate Garden Playground

I was the most surprised guy in town — that town being Wellesley, Ontario. It is the place that made apple butter famous. I was there one May weekend for a fish fry, which might lead you to suspect that there is a large body of water nearby. Not so. But there must be a great fishmonger because more than 350 people showed up to sample the fish — the best I had tasted in some time.

The surprise came the next morning. Between breakfast with 20 of the local Home Hardware staff and my store appearance, I wandered down, at the invitation of the owner, Shauna Leis, to a neat little home in town with the most extraordinary garden. I was invited to view the family's outdoor space, which had been designed almost exclusively for kids. Check out the accompanying photos to see what I mean.

As I entered through the back, just beyond the garage, I was greeted by a fort, shaped like a pirate ship. A pirate ship! The kids, Erik (5) and Megan (8), designed it themselves, with some help from their daddy, Kirk Bergey, no doubt. To suggest that this is the dream of any youngster might be an understatement. Here, on their own ship, they act out their fantasies with neighbours and friends through creative play.

The ship was just the beginning: beyond it was a "grotto" where hobbits live (they say) and when the hobbits don't inhabit the hobbit house, Megan and Erik do. The door is a little over a metre high, so most adults are discouraged to climb in. Buried, as it is, under a few metres of soil, the hobbit house is cool in summer and fun year-round.

Both Erik and Megan have their own veggie garden.

The garden includes a fire pit, for marshmallow roasts (and sing-alongs), a nature trail (down to the river), and a "flat" where everyone in the family plays soccer and badminton in the summer and hockey on the homemade rink in the winter.

Shauna and daughter Megan show off their homemade pirate ship (bottom) and "hobbit house" (top). ↑

Managed Disrepair

To suggest that Erik and Megan are lucky is to discount the contribution that they both made to designing their outdoor nature/garden space and the time that they take to maintain it in a special state of managed disrepair (my words). You see, if you want the fox to trot through your garden, the rabbits to munch on your dandelions, and the frogs to jump into the puddles, you have to know one thing about Mother Nature — a "perfect" environment doesn't work so well. It has to be just a bit messy; intentionally messy.

Anyone who has read the book *Last Child in the Woods* by Richard Louv knows the term "nature deficit disorder." This is what happens when children grow up without a connection to the natural world around them. When square walls, electrical outlets, and (dare I say it) computers dominate a child's life, he or she becomes disconnected from nature. Chances are, if a child is not introduced to the wonders of nature, he or she won't likely discover it as they mature into adults. Worms are "icky," bugs are "bad," and dirt is, well, dirty. Kids who make their own mud pies and watch the chrysalis from a caterpillar blossom into a monarch butterfly know differently.

Kids who know nature enjoy a form of wealth that travels with them throughout their lives. It is a different form of wealth: one that has nothing to do with money.

It is my opinion that we are reversing that curve as more parents engage their children in outdoor play. The local park, conservation area, cottages, and, indeed, the backyard garden, provide a host of opportunities for us to enlighten and engage young people in an experience that cannot be replicated indoors.

The rewards, short- and long-term, are enormous.

The next section will provide you with a starting point. You know your kids better than anyone, so tailor the activities to them. Try some of my suggestions, or put on your own creativity hat and design some projects yourself.

 **PROJECTS**

As our children get older, different parts of their brains and bodies start to develop. It's important not to overwhelm a younger child with complex ideas, and for older children, keeping them interested is part of figuring out how complex to make the subject matter. But you can work with your child, no matter their age.

Keep in mind that every child is different, so start with the guidelines here and modify them as you see fit. The main goal is to keep them engaged. Perhaps, one of your children prefers to plant seeds and watch them grow and another prefers to study the bugs that visit the gardens. Tailor the activities to your child's interests and show interest of your own. Let your child learn and explore; let them teach you.

I've broken down this section into ten of my favourite garden concepts and paired them up with a few projects for different age groups. Mix and match, do them all, or use them as inspiration to create your own activities. Have fun and be creative. You're bound to learn just as much as your kids will.

Project #1: Monarchs

More and more insect species are being put at risk, the vast majority due to habitat destruction and the use of agricultural pest controls. As parents (and gardeners), we can encourage our kids to understand the consequences of losing species and give them interactive projects to keep them interested in conservation efforts. Monarchs are a great place to start: they are visually appealing, won't bite or sting, and are found throughout Canada.

Kids

Plant milkweed. This is fairly easy, but requires a little patience or some "behind-the-scenes" prep work from you. Milkweed seeds need what is known as cold-moist stratification. This essentially means they need to experience winter in order to germinate. For you, this means you need to put the seeds into some moist soil and put the whole lot into the fridge for six weeks.

Once they've received their "winter treatment," you can explain how the seeds will germinate (keep a few extra handy to show the little ones — they are large seeds easily handled by awkward hands). Once they start to sprout, well, then the real excitement begins. You'll be able to watch them grow and eventually plant them out.

Your other option is to give it a real Canadian winter. Pot up some seeds with the kids in the fall and put them outdoors in a place that won't be disturbed. It's okay if they get snowed on and they will most definitely freeze — that's also okay! It's what would happen if they fell from the plant anyway. They'll germinate come spring.

A monarch enjoys the pollen and nectar of rudbeckia. →

Youth

If you've planted some milkweed in your yard, chances are good that you'll have monarch visitors at some point in the summer. They start showing up at my place in June, but it will vary depending how far north you are.

This is a good time to start teaching older kids about the monarch life cycle. It really is fascinating how something as small and seemingly fragile as a butterfly can make the 2,500-kilometre journey from Canada to Mexico.

If you don't have your own milkweed, you can usually find some in open fields nearby (harvest only the seeds in late fall, as the plants are rhizomatic and will not survive if you dig them up). There's also a good chance you'll find seeds at your local garden retailer. As your milkweed matures, look on the undersides of the leaves for small whitish-yellow eggs in early summer. There will likely be many on one leaf, but they will not be clustered together. Visit the

MONARCH LIFE CYCLE

The monarch life cycle is incredible when you really think about it. Like the chicken and the egg debate, there isn't one correct place to start, so I'll just pick a spot.

The Beginning

Monarch babies are born from eggs. They emerge as tiny white caterpillars with black heads and immediately begin to pack on the kilos … or milligrams. They're only tiny after all. After only a few days, the caterpillars have developed the classic white, yellow, and black stripes. About two weeks of constant feeding will leave the caterpillars plump and ready to change.

The Change

If you've ever watched a caterpillar change into a chrysalis, you know it's a rather violent experience. Imagine yourself wearing a straight jacket with a zipper in the back. Your arms are no help and you have no choice but to wiggle your way out. That is essentially what the monarch caterpillar must do. With a good deal of swaying back and forth, the colourful outer skin is shed and by the end of the ordeal, that skin is a crumpled ball below a shiny chrysalis. That chrysalis will undergo major changes over the next two weeks, transforming

from an opaque shiny green to a translucent shell that exposes the black and orange wings underneath.

The Final Stage

Emerging from the protective covering is not nearly as difficult as getting into it. The clear shell cracks and the butterfly begins to push its way out. The wings are folded at first, crumpled to fit into the tiny space. Over about an hour, the wings dry out and crisp up. It can take several hours before the butterfly is ready for his or her first flight. He or she will find a mate and new eggs will be laid upon a milkweed leaf.

The Last Generation

The last generation of the year is a little different. They are actually born without functional reproductive organs and, instead of mating, spend the remaining days before their journey drinking as much nectar as they can. The cooler temperatures signal the mass movement of butterflies. Once they've reached Mexico (about two months later), the warm temperatures initiate the development of reproductive organs and the butterflies will mate. The first eggs will be laid in March on the journey back north.

The monarch chrysalis → is a brilliant green flecked with a gold and black ridge.

milkweed frequently to look for the very recognizable yellow, black, and white caterpillars. Take pictures and watch them grow, but understand that monarchs don't waste any time. You're looking at a maximum of 20 days from hatching to chrysalis. They grow quickly (a rewarding experience for a young enthusiastic kid).

You're not likely to see the chrysalis hanging from a milkweed plant, but that doesn't mean they're not around. Poke around (carefully) in the area. You're looking for a shiny green torpedo-shaped shell. Don't get too frustrated if you can't find any: the benefit here is that the caterpillar has done a really good job of protecting him (or her) self and you can use this as an opportunity to explain why this is important.

Visit the area in another week or two and you'll start seeing the butterflies in flight, perhaps looking for food or a mate, depending on the time of year.

↑ A community butterfly garden.

Teens

If your child as a teenager is still interested in monarchs, woohoo! Give yourself a pat on the back. If not, that's okay: there are lots of other aspects of the gardening world for them to take a liking to and the chances are good that an interest in monarchs and other features of nature's world will redevelop later in life. It never ceases to surprise me how long an interest in gardening can lie dormant within an adult, emerging when life provides the opportunity for it to bloom (pardon the pun).

When a budding naturalist or gardener is in his or her teens, it's important to see the bigger picture. Yes, monarchs are great and their lifecycle is fascinating, but teenagers are looking for a call to action. They're looking to get others involved. Encourage them to form a group at school or within the community. Bring like-minded neighbours and students together and begin a food or pollinator garden. Be sure to make this a special, social, and fun time.

Here are a few ideas to get you started:

- Research the different milkweed types (there are plenty to choose from) and determine which would be best for your area. Use this information to educate the community and encourage others to add it to their gardens.

- Fundraise and buy milkweed seeds. Germinate them yourselves at home and pass them out or offer to plant them at no cost to neighbours, schools, churches, or public parks. Remember: if the property doesn't belong to you, ask permission to plant.

- Take it to a higher level. Go to a ward councillor or municipal council with a plan (maybe there's unused public space in your community where you'd like to see a butterfly and hummingbird garden). This can be a good way to encourage kids to involve themselves in government. Even if they never run for office, they will see the importance of listening to political platforms and, especially, the importance of voting. When they can have their voices heard, there's motivation to elect someone who will listen.

↑ Milkweed pods, almost ready to open.

Project #2: Birds

Birds are great for kids of any age and the hobby often sticks well into adulthood. As kids get older, the complexity of the lessons can increase and diversify. We are fortunate in Canada to have as many bird species as we do and so many of them are easy to find either in the backyard or on a day trip to a local park or conservation area. Knowing what kinds of birds are native to your area is a huge help and I encourage you to do some research on your own first. There are so many North American bird guides around — pick one and go!

Kids

Encourage bird activity in the yard by planting sunflowers. The flowers themselves are quick to grow, providing a rewarding experience for an impatient little gardener. Choose a variety of shapes and sizes to make it interesting. All sunflowers will be monstrous to a kid, but I love seeing the look on their faces when meeting a Russian Giant (if you don't know, these plants can reach a height of five metres).

For best results, start your seeds in the ground outdoors after the threat of frost has passed. I would suggest setting out a separate space for sunflowers so it's easy for the little ones to see the

↑ Sunflowers are easy to grow, attract birds, and kids love their massive flowers.

plants growing. If that's not a possibility, you can certainly start them indoors and transplant them out — another fun activity. Once planted, you and the kids can enjoy the flowers throughout the summer and the birds will be attracted in the fall when the giant flower heads have put out seeds.

Youth

As the kids get older (and maybe a little bit rambunctious), you can use birdwatching as a quiet time activity. You can take this game anywhere you want and you can tailor the game to your child's preferences. A little behind-the-scenes prep work again will show your own interest. Believe it or not, kids pick up on that kind of stuff, and if you are interested, there is a much greater chance they will share that interest.

Do a little research on your own to find out which birds are popular in your area. Feeder birds are always a good choice. In Canada, you can expect to find chickadees, robins, blue jays, nuthatches, and cardinals with minimal effort. Use your list to make a checklist. Include pictures and a space to mark off how many they've seen. This not only teaches the kids about birds, but about math and patience as well.

If you're going to play this game, I would suggest putting up a couple of feeders in your yard. Use different seed in each and add a hummingbird feeder. This keeps the game interesting and keeps birds visiting the feeders.

Check out Bird Studies Canada for more great projects that kids will enjoy. BSC is the largest not-for-profit birding organization in the country and they have done a great job of generating interest in birding among young people. Look for Project Feeder Watch and the annual Great Canadian Birdathon among other activities. Kids can participate right at home and report their findings online. It is interactive, educational, and fun!

↑ Hummingbird feeder.

Teens

If your teenager is interested in birds and wood-working, I will suggest the obvious: build a nesting box, birdhouse, or feeder. Using non-treated lumber or barnboard, they can put together something that they can give away or use in their own yard.

Be sure to tailor your birdhouses to the birds that live in the area. I put up 27 bluebird boxes, desperately wanting them to make a happy home in my meadow. I wouldn't, however, suggest you do the same unless you also have a meadow. Bluebirds prefer open space surrounded by suitable nesting areas and unless you can provide that, your nesting boxes will sit empty. As it has turned out, I have not succeeded in attracting bluebirds, but I do have a healthy population of tree swallows and house sparrows! I don't mind this at all, as the swallows eat a huge number of mosquitoes and the sparrows have a great song that wakes me up in the mornings, especially during the spring.

Fortunately, there are many other birds that love to live in close quarters with the human population and have learned to thrive in the urban environment. Do some research, or have your teen do it, and find out which birds would appreciate a new urban home. Consult with Bird Studies Canada for valuable information. It comes down to finding a suitable plan. Remember that birds like different-sized houses and tailoring your design to the bird you wish to attract will increase your success rates dramatically.

Tree swallows, new parents, in my meadow. A great day! →

Project #3: Beneficial Bugs

The garden is teeming with life. Generally we think of the bug category as two (so very basic) subcategories: good bugs and bad bugs. We want the good and don't want the bad. Simple enough. As a parent and a gardener, though, you can teach your kids that there is more to the insect world than "good" and "bad." Every insect has a purpose, whether that purpose is pollination or food for another insect. Even wasps and mosquitoes have a purpose in the broader world of nature, despite the fact that they don't directly suit our purposes.

Kids

In my experience, most kids are interested in bugs at an early age, but at some point along the line they are taught to avoid them. Have you ever met a kid who didn't want to see a pill bug roll up into its tiny armadillo ball or a worm wriggle in the palm of their hand?

Teach kids bug basics: What makes a spider different from a beetle? How does a butterfly eat with its long straw-like tongue? How do worms make tunnels? How are ants able to carry 100 times their own body weight? The possibilities are endless and the fascination on the part of kids has no bounds.

While you're at it, teach them about an insect's body parts and how they differ from their own: how spiders have multiple sets of eyes; how butterflies smell with their feet; how worms have five hearts; how an ant's skeleton is on the outside of its body.

Instill interest rather than fear, but promote care and appreciation for the insect world. Yes, insects can bite and sting (and it will happen), but teach children that these are defence mechanisms and survival methods.

Youth

Older kids can start making the connection between the insect and its role in the ecosystem. In a similar fashion to the bird game mentioned previously, you can do a little prep work and prepare a beneficial insect ID card with photos. If you don't know your beneficial bugs very well, this will be a good learning experience for you, too.

The younger the kids are, the bigger the bugs should be. Start with lady bugs, soldier beetles, assassin bugs, dragon/damselflies, and spiders. The smaller and more nimble insects, like the green lacewing, red velvet mite, syrphid fly, tachnid fly, and thrip can wait until they are a bit older.

Many of these insects are attracted to edible plants like dill, fennel, legumes, and bolted lettuce. Tie in your vegetable garden plans with the beneficial insect observation. If you don't have space for a vegetable garden, consider starting a few dwarf dill seeds in a container. You really can't go wrong with dill where beneficial insects are concerned. Ditto for marigolds.

Teens

Insect hotels (or "insect condos" as I like to call them) are gaining in popularity here in Canada and have been used in European gardens for some time. Sure, you can buy them and they will look very nice in the garden, but you have to remember that bugs don't like "neat and tidy." They prefer a messy house with lots of hidey-holes so they can steer clear of predators and safely lay their eggs.

Teenagers who are crafty will enjoy this project. I built an insect condo in my yard a few years back and I absolutely love it. Each year I observe more

← Right (3 images): The ladybug lifecycle. Top left: A yellow garden spider (Argiope aurantia). Middle, bottom left: The life of a lacewing.

and more insect activity and no doubt I will continue to do so as the years roll on. The longer it sits there, the messier it will become and the more that bugs, toads, frogs, and the like will enjoy it.

Have your teen design and build one for your garden (ask for it as a gift for Mothers'/Fathers' Day!). Let them be creative and offer to help. To help you get started, here's a short list of some popular beneficial insects and the types of dwellings they'd prefer.

Lacewing: straw, grass clippings, and corrugated cardboard
Ladybeetle: bundled sticks and twigs
Beetles: sticks and rotting logs
Bees: bamboo canes and wood that has been drilled with various-sized holes (five to 10 millimetres is preferred and keep away predators)
Hover/Syrphid Fly: bundled sticks and twigs

There are lots of options for a backyard insect condo and the best materials are the ones you find in the yard anyway. It's an inexpensive and fun project with big results.

MY INSECT HOTEL

I assembled my insect hotel in one weekend. It consists of materials that I had on the property, so that other than a bag of sand, there was nothing that I needed to buy. Flat stones provided the framework and the structure. They sit on top of one another with a 1/2 centimetre of sand between each layer. Do not use mortar, as you want the seams to be loose and open. The middle portion I made in my woodworking shop using scrap wood. The holes are 3/8" to attract mason bees and the various hollow "straws" are stems from my meadow and from straw. The wood collection is loose, too: made up of small pieces, it will rot down fairly quickly. I pushed corrugated cardboard into open spaces in the hotel and lined up 4 bricks deep, 3 bricks wide at the base as winter habitat for snakes. I want and encourage snakes in my hotel to help control slugs and earwigs.

Try building a bug condo for yourself: use your imagination; check out the garden shed and garage for "stuff" that might work and perhaps you will end up with an interesting architectural feature in your garden as a result. At the very least you will have a conversation starter for visiting guests!

Project #4: Composting

I see a composter and its contents much the same way that a chef sees a counter of great food: ingredients for a fabulous meal. Before the chef gets to work preparing a meal, they visualize the meal that they are creating.

I do the same thing with compost: my "meal," however, is a fabulous garden rather than a filet mignon.

I love my backyard composter. I love that I don't have to rely on city services to ensure my organic food waste is being diverted from landfill. And I love adding the finished material to my gardens. Composting is more than just diverting food scraps away from the garbage bin, though. It's a delicate balance between nitrogen, carbon, and a whole host of insect decomposers.

Kids

Kids are impressionable. You were. I was. It's how we learn. Starting to teach the basics of composting at a young age can make a huge difference in your child's values as they grow up. I believe we need to move away from the "throw-away" society we are living in and move toward a more

↑ There are many benefits to installing a backyard composter.

↑ Get kids involved in the composting process.

sustainable one. Introducing kids to composting is a step in the right direction.

From a very young age, we learn that food keeps us alive. What is often not passed along is that the banana peel, although not tasty for you, is tasty for something else. That banana peel will keep something else alive. At a younger age, though, we don't want to be bombarding our kids with heavy topics like decomposition and sustainability: we need to teach them through our own actions.

Don't have a composter? Start one. It can be as simple or as complex as you wish — just make it work for you. Then teach your children the basics: what can go into a composter, what happens to the stuff you throw in, and why it's important to compost the material that you do. From there, it's all about repetition and teaching by doing. Give the kids the job of taking food scraps to the bin; while making dinner, ask them where various scraps should go. Involve them as much as possible and, in time, you will see that they just take for granted that composting is part of day-to-day life: we create waste, which is used as a resource to produce more food in the garden. Simple. But only if you practise.

Youth

Older kids will be able to comprehend the finer details behind composting: that is, the process of decay. Experiment with different organic materials in the composter. Watch how they break down and take note of any insects that are helping with the process. If you can, compare the decomposition of, say, an apple core in two environments: inside the composting environment and outside of it. It won't take long for you (and the kids) to realize that inside the composter the material "disappears" a lot quicker.

If you work closely with your child's school, this might be a good age to introduce the concept there. In recent years I have seen an explosion of interest in schoolyard composting, so the idea isn't entirely out to lunch. Suggest a vermicomposter (composting with worms) and offer to help build one. The worms provide a visual for the kids and they learn that their organic lunch material has a larger purpose. Vermicomposter kits are also available and not difficult to find.

Teens

Have the older kids build you a vermicomposter. There are lots of options here. If you have a teenager who is handy, ask them to build one themselves or help you make one. If they aren't handy or you don't have access to tools, ask around. There are likely neighbours or community groups that will have tools and would be more than willing to teach the skills to use them. If you have younger kids or aren't that handy yourself, approach the local high school about building one for either their own school or for a grade school nearby. Offer to help with the research (there are so many types out there and it will depend on space and the amount of available organic material).

There are numerous composting options out there. Anything from the two-tiered/split-level wooden worm haven (see page 206 for instructions) to the side-to-side plastic bin, which works just as well. And, of course, the regular old-fashioned composter like I have: just a box that I put the organics into. Use what you like best! Keep in mind that optimal heat generation in a composting unit is achieved in a four-by-four-foot (1.2-metre x 1.2-metre) container. Nailing four skids together works quite well!

Project #5: Bats

Bats have a bad reputation. We all know them for their attic-dwelling ways and Hollywood has made them out to be vampires whose sole purpose in life is to get tangled in your hair and suck your blood. I am here to tell you that most of the tales are bunk and that these flying rodents are much more than that. True, they can be pests in the attic if they get in, but in Canada you can forget about them swooping at your head in search of a meal: the species that are native to our country just don't do that. The vampire bat is a real thing, but is nowhere near as menacing as Hollywood wants you to believe. And they don't exist here, anyway.

Kids

Because bats aren't the most visible of mammals, preferring to come out at night, the easiest way to teach your child about them is to read books, watch videos, and visit nature centres. Sometimes nature centres will have taxidermy animals that provide really good visuals for young kids.

Keep an eye out for learning sessions in your area. Remember that your kids will often be afraid of the same things you are. If you absolutely cannot stand the thought of attending a bat exhibit or evening event, arrange for another adult to go with them. And, if the thought of doing any of those things is not something your child can handle, consider asking them if they want to bring a friend. Or, just stick to the videos and taxidermy for the time being.

Youth

This is when we can start teaching our kids the benefits of bats. Mention how they eat several thousand insects every night and that nursing brown bats can eat more than their own body weight during the same period. If your child isn't fond of mosquito bites (who is?), make sure to let them know that they are one of the most popular snacks for the native brown bat. Share other fascinating facts: bats sleep upside down; most aren't actually blind and can see very well; some capture insects in their wings, using them like a net; tiny brown bats can live for 40 years; and they can hibernate for seven months of the year. Bats are seriously amazing creatures. If you have an inquisitive child, you may end up learning all these things from them!

At this age (between eight and twelve), you might have better luck getting them out to a bat watch, and it certainly doesn't hurt that they get to stay up past their usual bed time either!

Teens

By their teenage years, some kids will simply know that bats exist and others will be much more familiar. Encourage them to build a bat box. They are fairly easy to build and can make a fun project. Instructions for building your own bat box can be found on page 208.

Bat boxes need to be hung at least four metres in the air (six metres is better). If you don't have the space, ask a neighbour or relative if they do. They'll appreciate the gesture — and the less frequent mosquito bites, I'm sure.

Once again, you can make this a community or school experience, with your teen being the expert on the matter. It will give them confidence speaking in groups and very important teaching and researching skills.

A note about bat houses: they should not be hung in trees. A six-metre radius of clearance is important; that is, no trees or other obstructions within that space. This aids in keeping with a direct path to and from the house and deters predators that like to sit and wait for bats to return. Bats like to be warm: keep the bat house in an area that will receive six to eight hours of sunlight a day.

When researching bat boxes, the main difference you will find between them is the size. If you're in an urban setting, you likely won't need a very large box (at least to start). Most bat boxes that I have ever seen are constructed using the same basic design, using barnboard or another type of roughed-up wood so the bats have something to latch onto. The landing pad on the bottom of the bat box is one of the most important features. Bats aren't the best where landing is concerned, so the size and type of material should be chosen to assist them. Choose your materials carefully and never use treated wood.

Project #6: Trees

The decline of the urban tree canopy across Canada is real. In Toronto, trees covered 40 percent of the land in the 1960s; that number is now less than 25 percent. In Ottawa, more than 20 percent of the tree canopy was lost to the emerald ash borer between 2013 and 2016. As the volunteer chair of Trees for Life, the urban tree coalition, I know all too well the benefits that trees provide to our cities and our landscape in general. Studies have shown that trees reduce crime, encourage pedestrian traffic, slow vehicular traffic, reduce erosion and flooding, reduce heating and cooling costs in winter and summer, respectively, and increase property value and tourism. And that's just the beginning.

Kids

Kids (hopefully) see trees every day. Maybe not many, but it's likely that your street has a few planted in that city-owned space between the road and the sidewalk. What kids don't often do is think about trees. I know it's cliché, but they are taken for granted. Take the time to point out the different kinds of trees. In the fall, pick up seeds (maple keys make great little helicopters), use fallen leaves to ID trees, and explain how trees are

a habitat for a number of creatures. On rainy days, I always enjoyed putting leaves under some paper and using a crayon to colour over the area. You can see all of the veins and imperfections so clearly.

Locate a pick-your-own farm with orchard trees (apples, pears, cherries, for example). Visit in the spring when the trees are in full bloom. The scent itself is enough motivation for me, but you can use it to show your little ones pollination in action. Then return to visit during harvest. The miracle of fruit production that occurs in the meantime is worthy of more than a few dinnertime conversations!

Youth

A lot of tree seeds will germinate with very little effort. Think about how many tree seedlings you see growing out of sidewalk cracks or in between rocks in your garden. It doesn't take much and this can be a good thing where kids are concerned. When kids are a bit older, have them collect seeds and pot them up. The soft fruit seeds, like maple and birch, will germinate faster than the hard-shelled ones like walnut and oak. Once germinated and nurtured into small saplings, you can help your child plant it out and care for it. This

↑ Art from nature.

kind of responsibility is important to instill at a young age and planting a tree is a fun way to do it; likely a memorable one as well.

Use the fall and winter to explore patterns in tree bark. You will likely see insect burrowing holes, maybe woodpecker holes, and knots (where tree branches used to be). Use sidewalk chalk to follow the ridges and ask if they can see any patterns.

If you have cone-producing evergreens nearby, collect a few dropped cones and bring them home to set up your very own weather station. Sitting them in a visible location outdoors will allow them to experience the subtle moisture changes in the air. The pine or spruce cone will open when moisture is low and close back up when moisture increases. The reason? Pinecone parents don't like competition. That is, light (dry) seeds will blow much farther from the parent tree and thus reduce competition for sunlight, nutrients, and water. And so, when the air is dry, the pinecones are encouraging seed dispersal by opening up.

Artistically inclined kids may want to express their interest in trees through various media: encourage it! Paint, pencil, sculpture, anything they can come up with. Let them be creative.

Teens

The teenage years are all about becoming who you will be: you are figuring out what you like, who you like, and who you like to associate with. It can be a scary time for a parent.

I generally find that people with an inherent appreciation for the natural world around them and how it functions are always inquisitive and just good down-to-earth [pun intended] people. To a large extent, the adult that we grow into is shaped during our teenage years, so it only makes sense to instill (or continue) a passion for trees and nature at this age. And who knows, it may produce some amazing fruit!

Look for local tree-planting or volunteer conservation groups. If your teen is even remotely interested in working in the out of doors, this is an excellent way for them to get experience and find out what they really like to do. Thanks to the Internet, finding like-minded people isn't hard. You'd be surprised at how many folks are out every weekend in your community making it a better place. You just have to find them.

If your teen is already making their way through school with the "outdoorsy types," encourage them to put together a group themselves and invite others in their school to participate in events. Maybe their school could use a few more trees in the yard; if so, help them put together a proposal to bring to the principal, help them raise funds to buy trees (lots of places will offer school discounts), and help them by promoting the event to your own friends (have them bring their kids!).

In my travels across the country, I often see fruit trees inhabiting the front yards of folks who couldn't care less that they produce a delicious crop at the end of the season. If that's your neighbourhood, see if your teen wants to do something about it. Approach your neighbours and ask them if they'd mind if the fruit was collected and donated to a good cause. Donate it to the food bank, pass it out to people who are less fortunate, or turn it into sauce and jams and sell them to raise money for a tree-planting event.

And finally, if you have the space, give them permission to grow their own tree. Ask them to assess the area first and use that information to choose a tree that will flourish in those conditions. If the space is small, suggest a dwarf tree; make sure they are considering future size and how that will impact the surrounding structures. There are a lot of things to consider and lots to learn. An excellent experience for a budding landscape architect.

← Collecting pine cones.

Project #7: Edible Flowers

Many of the flowers in our gardens are edible. Many are not. Consider taking an inventory of your garden plants and you might be surprised at how many can double as additions to your dinner plate. Edible flowers are not only palatable, they are visually stimulating. They add colour and unique flavour to a dish and are more than likely going to stimulate conversation at the table.

Kids

Young kids love to eat things they find. This can be a good thing (hey, they're trying new things) but can also be a little scary for parents. Knowing the plants in your garden will ease some of this fear, especially if you find that all of your garden plants are harmless.

Teach your kids when they are young that they can't just go eating anything they find. Establish rules for things like this and make it a habit to ask first. If you don't have anything edible in the garden, add some, then show your kids where they can go for a snack.

The following flowers not only make a splash in the garden, but they are guaranteed to be a hit with the little ones.

↑ Salad with marigold flowers. Nasturtiums and cosmos. →

- Tuberous begonias: leaves, stems, and flowers are edible. I find the flower petals are cool and refreshing like a cucumber with a slightly lemony aftertaste.
- Marigold: not my favourite smelling flower but their brightly coloured petals are an excellent addition to a salad. The flower petals are the only edible part, and I find them to be a bit peppery.
- Calendula: sometimes called "pot marigold." The flower petals are stunningly bright and look great on the plate.
- Nasturtium: this is a fun one to grow from seed. Fast germinating and quick to flower, they are very rewarding for young kids. Plus they taste good. Every part of the plant is edible and provides a peppery taste that some describe as being similar to a radish.

- Garlic scapes: if you've ever grown garlic, you will know that they put out a tall flower stalk early in the season (June for me). The flower actually draws energy from the bulb so it's best to cut them off. But don't throw them away! The entire scape can be eaten: they are often used in salads or chopped into potato dishes and soups.
- Carnations: the classic flower is rather sweet (kids love sweet things!). Remove the petals from the flower head for best results.

- Clover: I'm sure we've all chomped down on the sugary tube-like petals of the purple clover. You can eat the entire flower head, but I prefer just the petals.
- Mint: multiple varieties and flavours available including spearmint, peppermint, pineapple mint, and chocolate mint. A favourite for any kid to chew on, and you can add it to your afternoon drinks as well. Keep in mind that mint can be very aggressive, so it's best to keep this one in pots.

Roses, thyme, lavender, rosemary, bee balm, dandelion, and gladiola are all edible, as well. Plant them, let them grow, and add them to salads, drinks, or eat them raw.

Youth

When your kids are a little older, you can get them involved in the planting aspect of edible flowers. Set up a small patch and plant a few of the edibles mentioned above. Give them full snacking rights and some responsibility in the edible patch. Kids like to take ownership and there's a certain amount of pride when the plants start flowering. Of course, give them a hand and teach them about proper watering and weeding.

This would also be a good time to talk about plants you shouldn't eat. Rhododendron, castor beans (I would not grow castor beans in a garden accessed by kids), fruit from the bittersweet vine,

hydrangea, foxglove, delphinium, crocus, nightshade, and daffodil, are a few of the most common garden plants that are on the "do not eat" list. They are pretty to look at, but keep your distance.

Teens

You may not wish to admit it yet, but your teenager will eventually move out and have to fend for themselves. Among the plethora of jobs they'll have to start doing, cooking can be one of the most enjoyable. Unless that teenager is me, in which case, it just never happened.

Why not have your teen prepare a meal using the edible plants you have in the garden or in the pots on your balcony? If they aren't entirely familiar with the plants, help them out. Using the plants in a dish and having to research them a little bit can help them to remember all the names.

Foxglove. Beautiful to → look at, but beware: the entire plant is toxic, including the roots and seeds.

↑ Another plant to teach children to avoid: Hydrangea.

Project #8: Rainwater

The collection of natural rain water is a great way to encourage myriad species of wildlife to visit your garden. Collecting it to water your garden teaches the very basics of conservation. I have several rain barrels around my house and use the contents almost exclusively to water my flower gardens and all of my containerized plants during the gardening season. Rain barrel water is always warmer than tap water, it is soft, and after it falls from the sky it is charged with oxygen. Water that has been filtered will still contain oxygen, but the water molecules will have an altered shape that does not hold on to free-floating oxygen atoms as well. In short, go with the rain water. Your plants will love it.

Kids

I mentioned conservation earlier. The term is thrown around pretty loosely these days, but with good intention. It seems that everyone wants to conserve something, whether it be water, an animal or insect species, or an area of land. The movement is a good one. Good for us and good for the environment. We need to be teaching the basics of conservation to even the youngest children. Not letting the tap run when brushing your teeth; not flushing the toilet for no reason (and no, Mommy's necklace is not a good reason, but if you can get that through their heads, you have mastered parenting); recycling plastic, aluminum, paper, and cardboard; and using the composter.

Where outdoor watering is concerned, teach

← Ponds create habitat for frogs and other water-loving creatures.

kids how important water is to plants. Try plantng two easy-to-grow seeds (sunflower, for example). Keep one well-watered while you let the other one dry out after germinating. Talk about rain and how it affects plants. Go outdoors after a good rain and look at the plants. Ask your kids to describe the plants before and after the rain. Install a rain barrel and encourage kids to wash up using the rain water as opposed to running the tap indoors. It's fun, and the soft water will feel good on their skin. Consider placing a bucket under the tap to collect water and use it in your garden or for your containers.

Youth

The single most impactful project that you can undertake in the garden to benefit the environment and enhance biodiversity is to create a water feature. When your kids get a little older, you will be able to impress upon them the importance of standing water by installing a "watering hole." This doesn't have to be a big ordeal, and it doesn't have to be expensive. A half barrel (short enough that they can see in) with a few oxygenating plants like inexpensive water lettuce or water hyacinths will attract a variety of water-loving insects: the dragonflies are a favourite in my garden. If you'd like to add fish to the mix, choose inexpensive goldfish or an equivalent that doesn't need heated water to survive.

Continue to promote the use of the rain barrel, and if your young charges have a garden of their own, have them use that water instead of taking it from the tap. You can start to introduce the concept of oxygenation and how important oxygen is for plants. Like you and I, plants need it.

Visit a local pond and look for frogs and their tadpoles, watch dragonflies and fish. Ask your child to point out all of the living creatures they can see and what they can hear. This activity requires some patience, but it can be very rewarding, especially if a dragonfly lands on them while they're sitting quietly.

NATURE ORGANIZATIONS

If you're not sure where to begin when it comes to nature organizations that your teen may be interested in, here is a list of a few. It's just a start, but it's a good start. Remember that your local community may have its own groups that would be great starting places for the kids.

- Bird Studies Canada: www.birdscanada.org
- Canadian Wildlife Federation: www.cwf-fcf.org
- David Suzuki Foundation: www.davidsuzuki.org
- Ducks Unlimited: www.ducks.ca
- Earth Day Canada: www.earthday.ca
- Green Communities Canada: www.greencommunitiescanada.org
- Highway of Heroes Tribute: hohtribute.ca
- National Audubon Society: www.audubon.org
- Nature Canada: www.naturecanada.ca
- Nature Conservancy of Canada: www.natureconservancy.ca
- Parks Canada: www.pc.gc.ca
- Pitch-In Canada: www.pitch-in.ca
- Sierra Club Canada: www.sierraclub.ca
- Stewardship Canada: www.landstewardship.org
- Trans Canada Trail Foundation: http://tctrail.ca
- Tree Canada Foundation: https://treecanada.ca

DRAGONFLIES

With two large compound eyes and four elongated wings working independently of one another, the dragonfly is one of the most precise pond predators out there. As young larvae that live completely underwater, they will consume primarily mosquito larvae (it's easy prey and there is always plenty to choose from); however, if the circumstances arise, they won't turn down a meal of a tadpole or small fish. That's right, I said fish. As adults, dragonflies are no less hungry, but their diets must change slightly. Because they have gone from waterlogged nymphs to airborne adults, they now consume adult mosquitoes, flies, spiders, midges, moths, and even butterflies. Closely related is the damselfly: think all of the characteristics of a dragonfly but slightly smaller, with wings held together and behind while at rest. These two species are incredibly beneficial to a pond ecosystem that naturally attracts mosquitoes.

A "soaker hose" sends → water right to the roots, and less is lost through evaporation.

The launch day of → the Highway of Heroes Living Tribute: 117,000 trees planted beside Highway 401, a living tribute to our war dead.

Teens

By the time we are teenagers, we have learned about the water cycle, how water is moved from the various water bodies into the atmosphere through evaporation, how the water vapour collects to form clouds through condensation, and how the water droplets fall back down to Earth through precipitation.

You must continue to reinforce the importance of not wasting this resource. Introduce other water-saving technologies in your home and in your garden. A bleeding hose or "soaker hose" will decrease immediate evaporation of water, sending it right to the roots where it can be used by the plant; use drought-tolerant plants if your part of the country doesn't receive that much rain or gets unusually hot (check out *xeriscaping* for more information on the subject); teach the importance of watering deeply, which encourages the roots to travel downward in search of water, thereby creating plants that are able to survive mild droughts; and, finally, don't instill the obsessive need to have a green lawn year-round. For the most part, lawns will go brown in Canada. It happens, and your lawn is not dead. It will "wake up" and come out of summer dormancy when evening temperatures drop in August and morning dew becomes heavier. Water conservation is more important than a green lawn, and you'll be happy to know that when September rolls around, your lawn will green up again.

Where ponds and watering holes are concerned, a teenager will have a better grasp of the diversity that lies within. Encourage them to join a local conservation club or start their own if there isn't one nearby. They can organize pond and stream cleanups, tree-planting days, and awareness sessions where they talk to the community about water and soil conservation, pollution, and local wildlife concerns.

Project #9: Vegetables

Vegetable gardening has to be one of the most rewarding experiences: not only do you get to plant and watch everything grow, but there is a tasty reward at the end of it all. And vegetable gardening has come a long way in recent years. With the introduction of new "container varieties," we can grow just about anything even in the smallest of spaces. It's also a great way to get kids to eat their vegetables, although the jury is still out on Brussels sprouts (who came up with the idea that these were edible? Or is it just me?).

Kids

Kids are genetically programmed to want things to happen in a hurry. That is why sowing seeds that germinate and produce a crop quickly makes perfect sense. Beans, radishes, leaf lettuce, zucchini, and onions germinate quickly enough to keep their attention and mature to harvest in no time.

If your kid loves carrots, and, from my experience, most do, plant those in addition to some quick to germinate seeds so they don't lose interest (carrots take a full growing season to reach maturity). Mix the small carrot seeds with dry sand to help disperse them evenly over the soil.

↑ Bean seedling.

For a real hit, plant peanuts. Fresh roasted peanuts can't even compare to the store-bought variety. You'll love the bright yellow flowers and your kids will love digging up the string of peanuts come autumn. And the best part? You can grow them in a bushel basket–sized container or in the ground. Perfect for any home! Roast them in the oven at 350°F for 20 to 25 minutes.

If you grow a vegetable garden, let your children help out, and don't just give them the weeding tasks. Make their job seem important. Tie it in to the watering discussion we just had.

Youth

Here's where the real fun can begin: give the older kids their own garden patch or set of containers. Let them choose what they want to grow and help out when they need it. Teach by showing rather than telling, and never get upset if something doesn't work out. Remember, ***there is no such thing as failure in the garden, only composting opportunities.***

If you have the space, ask them to grow a little extra for a neighbour or local food charity. And when it comes time to deliver it, go with them but have them deliver the package. You will see your kid's eyes light up and see the pride they feel while passing it over, knowing that it's going to someone who needs it.

Teens

The local, or slow, food movement is a growing concept; the idea being that we eat food that was grown closer to home, support local farmers, discourage long-distance travel from farm to plate, and generally foster a better understanding of where our food comes from and the work it takes to grow what we eat. These ideas are more mainstream than ever before, and I don't see that trend changing.

Make a half-day trip to a local farmers' market with your teenager. I always find something delicious to snack on while I'm there and I always bring something home for dinner. It's fresh, local, often organic, and it just feels good to know I'm helping a neighbour.

If your teen is the entrepreneurial type or is mildly interested in lending a hand on a farm (maybe for some extra cash), the farmers' market is a great place to start. While many of them will have their workforce set out, you are more than likely to run into someone who is looking for some help. Your child will learn more than the basics of planting and harvesting and get a head start on their résumé.

I can tell you for certain that if they work on a farm for a summer they will learn the importance of discipline, planning, to be flexible (being prepared to change plans as the weather changes or equipment breaks down!) and, of course, they will learn a lot about the laws of nature. My many years in the retail business taught me that the number one mistake parents make when encouraging their own child to seek employment is asking employers on behalf of the kid. This almost never works. Most employers want to see the individual come in and apply of their own volition. Be helpful, but not overly helpful. Just saying.

↑ The farmers' market in Rouen, France. The appeal of fresh food is universal!

Project #10: Planting Native

The slow movement has been, I think, the cause for the surge in native plant sales. I'm talking not only about native plant seeds, but the offering of native plants at garden centres. I, for one, am glad to see it. Native plants attract native pollinators and provide a healthy habitat for so many other native insects. They are also accustomed to our Canadian climate, making them able to withstand our cold winters and droughty summers, when they are planted in similar growing zones as their native habitat.

Kids

As with milkweed, many native seeds don't germinate like the non-native seeds we buy from the stores. The plants have been growing in Canada for hundreds, if not thousands, of years: they love winter. Native plant seeds need winter, too; they need it to break down the seed coat so the seed can send its cotyledon (first green shoot) through and above the soil.

Unless you have very patient kids, I will suggest planting native seeds that don't require this process. You may not get a flower the first year from these species, but you'll get a plant. Try blanketflower and coreopsis: both have large seeds and will germinate fairly quickly. If you want to manage the expectations of your youngsters, start a few seeds several weeks before you start the project with your kids or buy transplants from your local garden retailer.

Take a walk through a native preserve or conservation area. Have your kids point out the flowers and any insect activity happening. Let them pick up leaves and just generally explore the outdoors and

↑ Laughter and delight are alive in the garden. Kids can teach us this.

ask them if they have some favourite species that they would like to grow in your home garden. Keep an eye on what they're getting into and avoid the poison ivy that will inevitably show up from time to time.

Youth

Bring together a few of the ideas we have already discussed: bees and pollination, non-bee pollinators, how native plants can reduce water consumption in the garden, and which native plants you can eat (for the older kids).

If you already have native plants in your garden, encourage older kids to count how many insects visit a certain type of native plant. Then have them do the same for a non-native plant. Are there any major differences? Talk about the kinds of insects that visit and the different types of bees you see.

Finally, while out on walks, take an ID book with you. This will depend on your child's age, but you'd be surprised at how many can make the connection between the flower in real life and the one in the book. Spend some time learning about a different species every week. Doing a little research of your own will help and you'll find lots of interesting tidbits of information you can share with your youngster. Hint: many native plants are sole hosts for insect species (like the monarch-milkweed relationship).

Teens

Native plants require a little extra handling before the seeds will germinate. Challenge your teen to grow a number of different native species from seed using the refrigerator method and the outdoor sowing method. The germinated seeds can be added to your garden or you can give your teen his or her own area to start something. Let them be creative.

Encourage kids to take their knowledge to others. If you have a garden club or other community group that routinely plants areas around your neighbourhood, encourage your teen to get involved. This is especially helpful if you don't have a large garden space or a garden that is primarily in small containers. Many native plants don't really thrive in containers, since their roots need to grow deep to survive the hot months of July and August.

Extra seedlings can be sold to earn a little extra cash. Sometimes garden groups will hold plant sales or exchanges that your teen may be interested in participating in. They will find what they like doing, especially the older ones. For the younger teens, they won't ask, but I'm sure they'd appreciate a little help.

↓ Black-eyed Susans.

191

 **FINAL WORDS**

Gardening with your kids is exceptionally rewarding. Knowing that you are not only passing along knowledge you have gained over the years but learning along with them makes for a special bond between parent and child. I am still learning from my own children, now in their 20s and 30s, even the ones who did not "take up the trowel" as a career. And it will continue to be that way, something I couldn't be more thankful for. I can only hope that you can share your knowledge and outdoor experiences with your kids.

Teaching kids about gardening isn't just about having them plant seeds or do the weeding for you. The activities I mentioned are meant (for the most part) to be done together in the beginning and independently as they mature. Their understanding of the outdoors will change and no doubt will go well beyond the definition of "gardening." You know your kids better than anyone, so let them show you what they like and build on their experience from there.

The parallels between parenting and gardening are hard to deny. You raise your kids and your plants with the hope that they will mature into something beautiful; something that makes you proud to say, "Yep, I helped to make that happen." Sure, there are struggles, as there are in all aspects of life, but the rewards of succeeding push you to keep trying. In the end, you realize you weren't perfect but you were perfect for them. Unlike gardening, though, kids need your attention year round, and I think, as Canadians, and as avid gardeners, we appreciate a break from the garden. It gives us time to focus on our future gardeners.

A fascination with → so-called "little things" can lead to great life experiences.

I learn a thing or two about gardening from Shane and Liam. →

REFERENCES

CHAPTER 1

National Gardening Association Special Report, "Garden to Table," (2014).

Nollman, Jim, *Why We Garden: Cultivating a Sense of Pride*, Colorado: Sentient Publications (2005).

CHAPTER 2

Clayton, Susan, "Domesticated Nature: Motivations for Gardening and Perceptions of Environmental Impact," *Journal of Environmental Psychology* 27 (2007): 215–24.

Environment Canada and North American Bird Conservation Initiative Canada, "The State of Canada's Birds" (2012).

Convention on Biological Diversity: www.cbd.int.

Lindemann-Matthies, Petra, and Thomas Marty, "Does Ecological Gardening Increase Species Richness and Aesthetic Quality of a Garden?" *Biological Conservation* 159 (2013): 37–44.

Niinemets, Ulo, and Josep Peñuelas, "Gardening and Urban Landscaping: Significant Players in Global Change," *Trends in Plant Science* 13 (2) (2007): 1360–1385.

CHAPTER 3

D'Abundo, Michelle L., and Andrea M. Carden, "'Growing Wellness': The Possibility of Promoting Collective Wellness Through Community Garden Education Programs," *Community Development: Journal of the Community Development Society* 39(4) (2008): 83–94.

Alaimo, Katherine, Elizabeth Packnett, Richard A. Miles, and Daniel G. Kruger, "Fruit and Vegetable Intake Among Urban Community Gardeners," *Journal of Nutrition Education and Behavior* 40(2) (2008): 94–101.

Garrett, Amelia, and Michael A. Leeds, "The Economics of Community Gardening," *Easter Economic Journal* 42(2) (2014): 200–13.

Hawkins, Jemma J., Kathryn J. Thirlaway, Karianne Backx, and Deborah A. Clayton, "Allotment Gardening and Other Leisure Activities for Stress Reduction and Healthy Aging," *Hort Technology* 21(5) (2011): 577–85.

Heim, Stephanie, Jamie Stang, and Marjorie Ireland, "A Garden Pilot Project Enhances Fruit and Vegetable Consumption Among Children,"

Journal of the Academy of Nutrition and Dietetics 109(7) (2008): 1220–226.

Koch, S., T.M. Waliczek, and J.M. Zajicek, "The Effect of a Summer Garden Program on the Nutritional Knowledge, Attitudes, and Behaviors of Children," *Hort Technology* 16(4) (2006): 620–25.

Ohmer, Mary L., Pamela Meadowcroft, Kate Freed, and Ericka Lewis, "Community Gardening and Community Development: Individual, Social and Community Benefits of a Community Conservation Program," *Journal of Community Practice* 17(4) (2009): 377–99.

Okvat, Heather A., and Alex J. Zautra, "Community Gardening: A Parsimonious Path to Individual, Community, and Environmental Resilience," *American Journal of Community Psychology* 47 (2011): 374–87.

Pitt, Hannah, "Therapeutic Experiences of Community Gardens: Putting Flow in Its Place," *Health and Place* 27 (2014): 84–91.

Schmelzkopf, Karen, "Urban Community Gardens as Contested Space," *Geographical Review* 85(3) (1995): 364–81.

Wakefield, Sarah, Fiona Yeundall, Carolin Taron, Jennifer Reynolds, and Ana Skinner, "Growing Urban Health: Community Gardening in South-East Toronto," *Health Promotion International* 22(2) (2007): 92–101.

Zick, Catherine D., Ken R. Smith, Lori Kowaleski-Jones, Claire Uno, and Brittany J. Merrill, "Harvesting More Than Vegetables: The Potential Weight Control Benefits of Community Gardening," *American Journal of Public Health* 103(6) (2013): 1110–115.

CHAPTER 4

Blair, Dorothy, "The Child in the Garden: An Evaluative Review of the Benefits of School Gardening," *The Journal of Environmental Education* 40(2) (2009): 15–38.

Chobak, Azadeh, "A Healthy Dose of Green: A Prescription for a Healthy Population," *Trees Ontario* (2012).

RESOURCES

CHAPTER 1
Green Roofs

"Design Guidelines for Green Roofs," Steven Peck and Monica Kuhn: www.cmhc-schl.gc.ca/en/inpr/bude/himu/coedar/upload/Design-Guidelines-for-Green-Roofs.pdf.

"Green Roofs for Healthy Cities": www.greenroofs.org.

Green Roof Plants: A Resource and Planting Guide; Edmund Snodgrass; Timber Press, 2006.

Green Building Products: The GreenSpec® Guide to Residential Building Materials (3rd Edition); Alex Wilson, Mark Piepkorn; New Society Publishers, 2008.

The Green Roof Manual: A Professional Guide to Design, Installation, and Maintenance; Edmund Snodgrass; Timber Press, 2010.

CHAPTER 2
Invasive Species

Most provinces and territories have a website dedicated to the invasive species of the area. Some do not. If your province of territory does not, visit one of the websites that covers all of Canada for information.

Invasive Species Centre: www.invasivespeciescentre.ca

Nature Conservancy Canada: www.natureconservancy.ca

BY PROVINCE:

Alberta: www.abinvasives.ca

British Columbia: bcinvasives.ca

Iqaluit: www.caisn.ca/en/research

Manitoba: invasivespeciesmanitoba.com

Newfoundland/Labrador: www.env.gov.nl.ca

Northwest Territories: www.enr.gov.nt.ca

Nova Scotia: www.invasivespeciesns.ca

Ontario: www.invadingspecies.com

PEI: www.peiinvasives.ca

Saskatchewan: www.saskinvasives.ca

Yukon Territory: www.yukoninvasives.com

Moving Firewood

Canadian Food Inspection Agency: www.inspection.gc.ca

Choosing the Right Plants

Taming Wildflowers, Miriam Goldberger, St. Lynn's Press, 2014.

100 Easy-to-Grow Native Plants: For Canadian Gardens, Lorraine Johnson, Whitecap Books, 2011.

Grow Wild, Lorraine Johnson, Fulcrum Publishing, 1997.

EASTERN CANADA

Wildflowers of Nova Scotia, Todd Boland, Boulder Publications, 2014.

Wildflowers of Newfoundland and Labrador, Peter Scott, Boulder Publications, 2013.

Wildflowers of New Brunswick: Field Guide, Todd Boland, Boulder Publications, 2015.

Plants for Atlantic Gardens, Jodi DeLong, Nimbus Publishing, 2011.

CENTRAL CANADA

Forest Plants of Central Ontario, Brenda Chambers, Lone Pine Publishing, 1996.

The New Ontario Naturalized Garden, Lorraine Johnson, Whitecap Books, 2001.

Plants of Southern Ontario, Richard Dickenson, Lone Pine Publishing, 2014.

WESTERN CANADA

Wildflowers of the Rocky Mountains, George W Scotter, Whitecap Books, 2011.

Wildflowers of Edmonton and Central Alberta, France Royer, University of Alberta Press, 1996.

Wildflowers of Calgary and Southern Alberta, France Royer, University of Alberta Press, 1996.

Alberta Trees & Wildflowers: A Folding Pocket Guide to Familiar Species, James Kavanagh, Waterford Press, 2010.

For easy reference for the beginner wildflower gardener, look into the Wayside series by Linda Kershaw, published by Lone Pine Publishing:

Ontario Wildflowers: 101 Wayside Flowers, 2002.

Manitoba Wayside Wildflowers, 2003.

Alberta Wayside Wildflowers, 2003.

Saskatchewan Wayside Wildflowers, 2003.

Native and Nativar Research

www.pollinatorgardens.org

CHAPTER 3

Last Child in the Woods: Saving our Children from Nature Deficit Disorder, Richard Louv; Algonquin Books, 2008.

Communities in Bloom:
www.communitiesinbloom.ca

STARTING A GARDEN
PROPOSAL GUIDE

Step 1: Summarize Your Plan
Write a short paragraph, answering these questions:
- Why does your community need a garden?
- How would a garden benefit the community?
- What type of garden would best suit the needs of the community? Why?

Step 2: Benefits of a Garden
Outline the benefits of a community garden. Start general and delve into the finer details of your garden. Be sure to cover the following topics:
- Exercise
- Mental Health/Stress Relief
- Safety
- Aesthetics
- Learning

Step 3: Make Goals
Briefly outline what you want to achieve with your garden. The easiest way to make goals is to list them. Try for at least three.

Step 4: Determine a Budget
You will require some money to get started. Put together a simple budget to get an idea of how much you will need. Include: structural costs (for raised beds, fences, a tool shed), signage and marketing, plants, tools, etc.

Step 5: Reaching Your Goals
Determine HOW you will reach your goals.
- How will you encourage others to participate?
- How will you raise money to start/support the garden?

Step 6: Challenges
No project of this magnitude comes without challenges. What are yours? If you anticipate them, you can plan for them. It's much easier to be proactive than reactive, and it's a lot less stressful.

Step 6: Creating a Timeline
Write down the play-by-play as you see it now. Note that this guideline will most likely change and you should be open to these changes.

Step 7: Your Members
Get to know your members and help them get to know one another. Have each member write a short personal bio, including: who they are, their background in gardening, why they're interested in the project, and what they think they will bring to the project.

Step 8: Continuous Improvement
Remember to keep this proposal open to change. Alter it as you see fit and as new opportunities present themselves.

COMMUNITY

Thank you for choosing to garden with us! We hope you are as excited as we are to grow great food and contribute to our wonderful community. For your convenience, we have outlined a few rules that will keep all participants safe and happy. If you have any questions about any of the following, please don't hesitate to contact us at _____.

Beginning of Season
1. You will have at least one plant put into your garden by _____.
2. You will tend your plot, weeding and harvesting as necessary.
3. If your plot has not been planted by _____, it is understood that you have forfeited your plot and it will be given to another gardener.

Seasonal Maintenance
1. Plots and aisle ways will be tended and maintained on a regular basis.
2. A minimum of _____ hours a week will be spent by each individual gardener on their plot.
3. Should you require assistance or an unforeseen circumstance arises, please contact us at the number above.

End of Season
1. You will have your plot cleaned up by _____.
2. At the end of the season, you will put scraps into the composter, except those that have been affected by a disease.
3. Diseased plants will be gathered separately and disposed of appropriately.
4. Stakes, string, and any other non-organic matter will be removed from the plot.
5. Walk ways and surrounding area will be cleaned at the end of the season.

Meetings
1. Meetings will be held every _____.
2. Attendance at these meetings is necessary.
3. Meetings will outline the expectations for maintenance and clean up. Meetings will also be used to interact with other gardeners. On occasion, we may bring in guest speakers. You will be given prior notice for guest speakers and you are encouraged to bring a guest.

GARDEN RULES

Tools

1. Several tools have been provided for your use. You will return tools to the shed after use and notify us should a tool break or go missing.
2. You are free to bring your own tools but understand that they are your responsibility.

Control Methods

1. Chemicals are not permitted in any plot within this garden. You must use only organic methods.
2. If you are unsure if a chemical is allowed in your plot, you will contact us at the number above.
3. Barriers and compost are always welcome.

Guests, Children, and Pets

1. Guests and children are welcome; pets are not.
2. Guests must understand the rules and respect all garden plots, tools, and sitting areas.
3. Children must be supervised and taught to stay on pathways. They must not dig in other people's gardens or in the pathways.

DO NOT:

1. Bring sand or gravel into your plot
2. Leave large rocks in pathways
3. Plant woody trees or shrubs or any perennial plant in your plot
4. Plant large plants or those with a spreading habit without the consent of the neighbouring plot owners
5. Allow your plot to become overrun with weeds
6. Throw waste material into a neighbouring plot
7. Leave garden while hose is running on your plot

DO:

1. Remove diseased plants
2. Consult with other gardeners prior to planting anything that may affect their plot
3. Keep pathways clear
4. Respect other plots
5. Mulch with leaves, grass clippings, or weed-free straw to reduce water usage
6. Turn off water tightly and water for no more than ___ minutes per day
7. Compost your healthy organic materials — that material goes right back into your plots for next year
8. Have fun and learn from other gardeners!

BUILD YOUR OWN INSECT HOTEL

YOU WILL NEED:

1" x 6" x 8' (X1) untreated board
Wood screws
1" x 8" x 8' (X2) untreated board or a 4' x 4' sheet
of one-inch plywood

Hand or mitre saw
Jig saw
Drill and bits

INSTRUCTIONS

From the diagram, you will want to start with Section B:

1. Using the 1" x 8" x 4' untreated board or plywood, cut a piece 8" x 18".

2. Using the jig saw, cut out two holes as shown; cut them one inch away from either side, except at the back. This will fit inside Section A and act as the bottom of the top portion of the unit.

Build Section A:

1. From the 1" x 6" board, cut two 20" lengths (A1 and A2) and two 8" lengths (A3 and A4).

2. Screw together the four sides of section A, as shown, using Section B as a guide to keep it square. Pre-drill holes to reduce risk of wood splitting.

3. Screw Section B to the bottom of Section A. It will fit inside rather than sitting on the bottom. This ensures that the holes you made in Section B will not be showing when the unit is put together.

Build Section C:

1. Cut four lengths of 18" from the 1" x 8" board (C1, C2, C3, C4). If you are using plywood instead, cut four lengths of 18" x 7".

2. Cut two lengths of 18" x 3" (C5 and C6). I would suggest using the 1" x 6" board and cutting it in half to get two 3" pieces.

3. For C8, if you are using 1" x 8" board, cut two lengths of 15"; for those using plywood, cut a piece 16" x 15".

4. C7 is where you will stack your insect materials. You may decide to support this piece with two brackets (as shown in the diagram) or you may decide to attach that piece directly to the legs of the unit.

5. To assemble Section C, begin by attaching the C1 to C6. Then screw C7 to C2 and C3 (use the brackets if you wish). The distance from the bottom will depend on how large you want the insect condo part of your unit to be.

6. Attach C4 and C5 together. Attach the C1/C6 and C4/C5 pieces to the C2/C3/C7 central piece. Flip the unit on its front and screw C8 to the legs.

Put It Together:

1. Place the A/B portion of the unit on top of C. Screw the top into the bottom, keeping the back flush so the top section overhangs the bottom section by about an inch.

2. Fill the condo portion of the unit with twigs, rocks, pinecones, straw, bark, and anything else you want to use to attract insects. I buried mine a bit because it gets fairly windy where I live, however, you may choose to sit the entire thing on a few cored bricks to give snakes and toads a place to sleep. After placing your condo where it will live, fill the legs and top with a good-quality potting soil. Choose seeds and flowers and plant them in the top. Once in place, don't move it around too much. You want the insects and other critters to know that it's there. Replant with annuals in the spring or try your hand at perennials. Be creative!

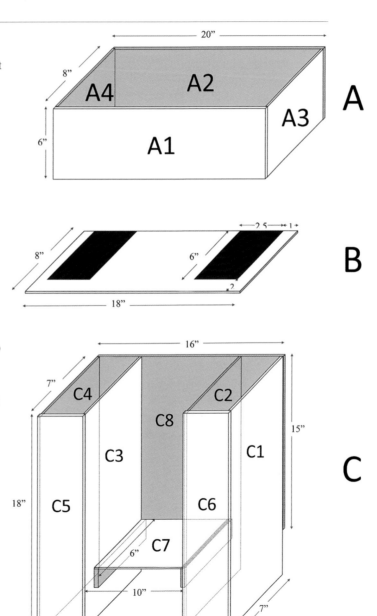

BUILD YOUR OWN VERMICOMPOSTER

YOU WILL NEED:

2" x 2" x 8' untreated wood

1" x 6" x 8' untreated boards (five of these)

4' x 4' piece of one-inch plywood

Wood screws

¼" chicken wire

Two hinges

Mitre saw or hand saw

Wire cutters

Drill and bits

Staple gun and staples

INSTRUCTIONS

For this vermicomposter, you are essentially building two boxes that will sit one on top of the other.

The Top Box (B):

1. Begin by cutting four lengths of 24" from the 1" x 6" board (B1 and B2).
2. From the same board, cut four lengths of 18" (B3 and B4).
3. Cut four lengths of 10" from the 2" x 2" wood.
4. Use wood screws to attach the two B3 boards to the first piece of 2" x 2", keeping it flush to the edge. Make sure you keep two inches from the bottom and one inch from the top. Keep a quarter-inch space between the boards to improve air flow through the interior.
5. Attach another length of 2" x 2" to the opposite side of the same set of boards (B3). Repeat for the opposite side of the box (B4). You will end up with two identical pieces.
6. Take two of the B1 boards and attach them to the sides of the box.
7. Finish by attaching the remaining two pieces of cut board (B2) and enclosing the box.
8. Cut a piece of chicken wire using the wire cutters. This will cover the bottom of the top box, attaching to the 2" x 2" corners and along the walls. Leave a little bit of excess so you have something to staple to the box. Fold and bend the chicken-wire panel into place. Staple and secure the piece, keeping all sharp edges away from the inside of the box.

The Bottom Box (C):

1. Cut four lengths of 24" from the 1" x 6" board (C1 and C2). From the same board, cut four lengths of 18" (C3 and C4).
2. Cut four lengths of 13" from the 2" x 2" wood. Create another box in the same way that you did for Box B. Note: keep the bottom of the 2" x 2" pieces flush with the bottom boards. The 2" x 2" pieces will stick up approximately 1 inch, which you will use to keep the top box from shifting when it is put in place.

Put It Together:

1. Once the bottom box (C) is built, put the top box (B) in place to ensure a good fit. Adjust as needed.

2. Create a bottom for the box (D) from a piece of the one-inch plywood (18" x 24"). Screw this piece to the corners of the box.

3. You may choose to add legs to the composter (I did and just used some scrap pieces of 2" x 4" each cut to about 3 inches in length).

4. To make the lid (A), cut three 24" lengths of 1" x 6" board. To keep these three pieces together as one piece and have it function as a lid, I used scrap-wood pieces (1" x 6" cut to 3" wide) and attached them to the boards as shown in the diagram. They don't have to be a certain length, just as long as they connect the three boards together. You want to keep a half inch of space between each board so your total lid width ends up being 19". Use two small hinges to attach the lid to the top box (B).

You will need to get worms for it to be a vermicomposter, or you can alter it slightly and avoid the worms all together by removing the chicken wire. You'll be able to remove the top box to easily access and turn the compost. If you're going to go that route, don't put a bottom on the box and have it sit directly on the ground to encourage insects to crawl in and help with the decomposition process.

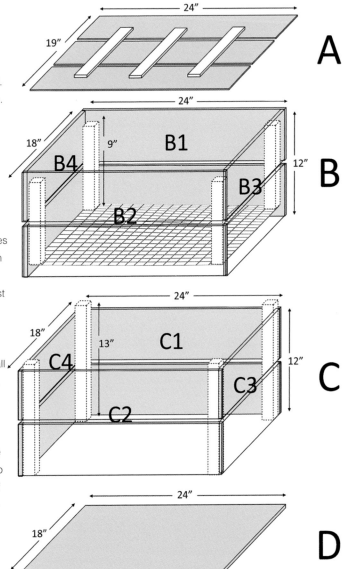

BUILD YOUR OWN BAT BOX

YOU WILL NEED:

4' x 4' x ½" exterior plywood or equivalent
  untreated board
1" x 4" x 6' board (untreated)
Window screen
2 shingles or black rolled roofing
Outdoor caulking

INSTRUCTIONS

From the plywood:

1. Cut a piece 24" x 18.5" (back — light blue in diagram)
2. Cut two pieces 14.5" x 17.5" (baffles — orange in diagram)
3. Cut one piece 5.5" x 18.5" (front bottom — dark blue in diagram)
4. Cut one piece 10.5" x 18.5", putting a 25° angle on the long edge (front top — green in diagram)
5. Cut one piece 6", putting a 65° angle along the long edge (top — red in diagram)

From the 1" board:

6. Cut one piece, 36" x 3.5". This will be used to create the two sides (grey in diagram). From one end of the board, mark 18" up along the left side. From the same end, mark 16.5 inches up along the right side. Draw a line between the two points. Cut.

7. Cut a hole in each of the side pieces, approximately 5" x ½", approximately 2.5" from the bottom of the board. Be sure you are cutting the hole along the edge that will be attached to the back of the bat box.
8. Cut four pieces 12" x ¾" (spacers — peach in the diagram)
9. Cut one piece 17.5" x ¾", putting a 65° angle on the top edge where it will meet with the roof (roof support — purple in diagram)
10. Cut one piece 17.5" x ¾", putting a 115° angle on the top edge where it will meet with the roof (roof support #2 — pink)

Put It Together:

1. Use a knife to scratch up the interior faces of the box. If using rough wood (such as barn board), this step is not necessary.
2. Lay the two front pieces flat on a table (green and dark blue). Put a ½" space between them. This will be used for air flow inside the bat house.
3. Take two spacers (peach) and place them ½" in from the sides and 1" from the bottom.
4. Using 1" wood screws, attach spacers to front pieces.
5. Take one baffle (orange) and place it flush with the spacers along the sides and approximately ½" longer than the bottom of the spacer.
6. Using 1" wood screws, attach baffle to spacers.
7. Line up two more spacers (peach) on top of baffle. Use 1" wood screws to attach to spacers.
8. Add the final baffle (orange) to the spacers, approximately 1.5" from the bottom of the front board (blue).
9. Place the second roof support (pink) flush with the front top piece (green). Ensure a flat surface for the roof to sit. Use 1" wood screws to secure in place.
10. Attach the roof support #1 (purple) to the roof (red), ensuring it is flush where it will touch the back and ½" from either side to allow room for the sides.
11. Attach the sides, using 1" wood screws that go through the spacers rather than the baffles.

12. Attach the roof to roof support #2 (pink) using a few screws.
13. Lay the unit face down with the top hanging off the side of the table.
14. Measure 4" from the bottom of the back, mark it on the back (light blue piece). Line up the bottom of the front with the line you just drew. This will give the bats a place to land before crawling into the bat house.
15. Supporting the back so it doesn't sag, attach the back piece to the roof support using a few screws.
16. Attach a piece of screen to the 4" landing pad at the bottom of the back piece (blue) and a few shingles or some black rolled roofing to the roof.
17. Hang your bat house and wait! You may have to get creative with the hanging depending on where it will go.

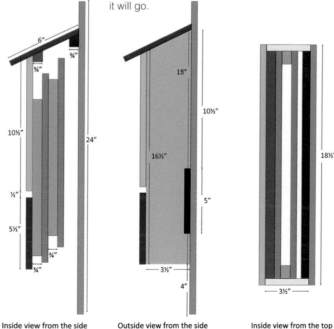

Inside view from the side   Outside view from the side   Inside view from the top

ACKNOWLEDGEMENTS

As I write this, I reflect on the three years since we began this journey. I say "we," as I have not done this alone.

First, my co-author, Marette Sharp, has made a contribution to this book that is palpable to anyone who knows my work. As the title implies, the word *new* suggests that this book offers a glimpse at the experience of horticulture in Canada that is both current and to some extent a view through a crystal ball. Marette has provided a youthful outlook on the world of gardening and a much clearer view of what the future may bring.

Marette was supposed to be my 20-something protegé, but, alas, as it turns out, it seems I am the protegé: a willing student of all that is new in the world of gardening.

I will take full responsibility for every word in this book, as every word passed through my filter of experience and knowledge. Primarily, this is my book, and any discrepancies or inaccuracies (could that even be possible?) rest on my shoulders. But, where credit is due, I share it with Marette. Where you read about bugs, pollinators, and biodiversity, you will hear the voice of a committed environmentalist. We share that commitment, Marette and I, but her voice is a particularly well-informed one.

Speaking of credit, a great deal of it must be shared with Brenda Hensley, my trusted assistant. In the final stages of the book's production, I called Brenda while vacationing in Boston to ask how it was going regarding the photos and final changes to the manuscript. In her usual style, she replied that all was under control and not to worry. From the beginning to the end of this project, Brenda has been there every step of the way. Who could ask for more?

My gardening hat is also off to Allison Hirst, our Dundurn editor. She is as thorough in her work as she is talented and creative. To Allison, designers Courtney Horner and Sarah Beaudin, our publicist Karen McMullin, and publisher Kirk Howard and his team, many thanks.

I'd like to extend a special thank-you to my book agent, Curtis Russell.

To my wife, Mary, and our four kids, thanks for being there, listening, and indulging me. Thanks for coaching, advising, and providing me strength. You do it so well.

And finally, thanks to my editor at the *Toronto Star*, Jane Van Der Voort. Jane has allowed me to "test drive" many of these concepts and ideas in my weekly column before they made it into permanent print in this book. Thanks, Jane!

PHOTO CREDITS

INDEX

Illustrations are indicated by page numbers in *italics*.

Visit us at

Dundurn.com
@dundurnpress
Facebook.com/dundurnpress
Pinterest.com/dundurnpress